Tata
A Voice from the Río Puerco

John—

Here's my father's life history in rural new mexico where el grew up. Hope you enjoy it.

Nasario

Nasario P. García, July 15, 1980.
Photograph by Isabel A. Rodríguez.

Tata
A Voice from the Río Puerco

COLLECTED AND EDITED BY
Nasario García

PUBLISHED IN COOPERATION WITH THE
HISTORICAL SOCIETY OF NEW MEXICO

UNIVERSITY OF NEW MEXICO PRESS
ALBUQUERQUE

Library of Congress Cataloging-in-Publication Data

García, Nasario P., 1912–
Tata : a voice from the Río Puerco / collected and edited by
Nasario García.—1st ed.
p.   cm.
Personal reminiscences of Nasario P. García, told in the
Spanish dialect of Río Puerco Valley, New Mexico, edited and
translated into English by his son.
"Published in cooperation with the Historical Society of New Mexico."
ISBN 0–8263–1519–4 (cloth).—ISBN 0–8263–1520–8 (pbk.)
1. Mexican Americans—Puerco River Valley (N.M. and Ariz.)—Social life and
customs.   2. Mexican Americans—Puerco River Valley (N.M. and Ariz.)—
Folklore.   3. Puerco River Valley (N.M. and Ariz.)—Social life and customs.
4. Tales—Puerco River Valley (N.M. and Ariz.) I. García, Nasario. II. Title.
F802.P83G37   1994
978.9'91—dc20
94–8241
CIP

To My
Brothers and Sisters
Beltrán, Juanito, Julia,
Elsie, Terry, Antoinette,
and Randolph

Contents

Glossary

Modismos/Idioms

Acknowledgments

Tata: A Voice from the Río Puerco, like *Recuerdos de los viejitos* and *Abuelitos* before it, both published by the University of New Mexico Press in collaboration with the Historical Society of New Mexico, has seen the light principally due to many people who have encouraged and supported my work. One voice in particular that assumed a special quality for me throughout the years was that of the late Myra Ellen Jenkins. I will miss her kind and enthusiastic support. I am equally indebted to Spencer Wilson and John Conron, Publications Committee, Historical Society of New Mexico. Since no work reaches maturity without the critical eye of an editor, I should like to salute Barbara Guth of the University of New Mexico Press and the other staff for their high professional standards.

Foreword

This is the third volume in Nasario García's trilogy on the life and times of the people of the Río Puerco valley of New Mexico. In all three works García has drawn on the experiences of those people who migrated from the Río Grande valley to the Río Puerco in search of land and a livelihood, first in colonial times and again in the late nineteenth century. In the two previous volumes, *Abuelitos* and *Recuerdos*, García collected and edited the stories of friends and relatives in the little communities of Guadalupe (Ojo del Padre), Cabezon (La Posta), Casa Salazar, and San Luis. From their memories he built a picture of daily life in those remote villages as well as preserving their archaic Spanish.

In this book García mines the stories of his father to provide one man's memories of rural Hispanic life in the early twentieth century. Indeed, these stories may well have been the beginning of García's work. His student days in Spain inspired the interviews with relatives, which in turn led to the stories of his father. To his credit, García did what too many of us did not do, record the memories of the old folks before it was too late. How many of us rue the day we were not smart enough to record our seniors and put their stories down? "If I had only thought to ask questions when they were alive" is a familiar lament. These stories are recorded verbatim, which gives them the authenticity of an old man regaling a son with tall tales and true. It is a fitting end to this series.

The Historical Society of New Mexico, through the Publications Committee, is pleased to include this work of Nasario García among the other volumes published through the co-publication agreement with the University of New Mexico Press. Members of the Committee

were the late Myra Ellen Jenkins, John P. Conron, and Spencer Wilson. The officers of the Society are: John W. Grassham, President; Robert J. Torrez, First Vice President; Darlis A. Miller, Second Vice President; Andres Segura, Secretary; and Carol A. Myers, Treasurer. The board members are: John O. Baxter, Susan Berry, Thomas E. Chavez, John P. Conron, Richard N. Ellis, Elvis E. Fleming, Austin Hoover, Margaret E. McDonald, Riley Parker, Agnesa Reeve, Carl D. Sheppard, David Townsend, Robert R. White, John P. Wilson, and Spencer Wilson.

Spencer Wilson
Historical Society of New Mexico

Preface

"Nos estamos acabando," the *anciano* said to Nasario García—"We're dying out."

The elder was explaining why he was telling his stories to his friend from the university with the tape recorder. But with those three words he also summed up the importance of Nasario's ongoing work to record the oral tradition of the people of the Río Puerco.

An oral tradition, by definition, is always at risk, as it relies upon the ears of each new generation. If unheard, the spoken word vanishes in the wind; listening keeps the story alive so it can be told again.

The oral tradition in New Mexico and the Hispanic Southwest, which has endured for centuries, is now in danger of dying with the old ones because so few of the young have wanted, or, indeed, been able to listen.

Nasario, however, has listened, and in his two previous works, *Recuerdos de los viejitos* and *Abuelitos*, he has reinforced the link to the past by committing those fragile spoken words to the printed page. By insisting on publishing those words of the *ancianos* exactly as they were spoken, Nasario has guaranteed that only the thinnest of pages comes between the storyteller and we who listen through our reading.

As a result, there is an intimacy in our reading of Nasario's books: we feel as though we are at the kitchen table, out in the corral, in front of the fireplace, listening to these aged and lyrical voices describe life in another time.

In *Tata* we have Nasario's most intimate and personal book. Based on a dozen years of interviews with his father, this book provides a wide-ranging record of traditions,

customs, and everyday life in the rural Hispanic village of the early part of this century. Yet as telling as the story is the voice that tells it, this honest, dignified, and often humorous voice of don Nasario that speaks so vividly on every page.

To read these pages is to listen along with the younger Nasario, as his elder namesake recreates a universe full of pride, spirituality, tragedy, and fun. He leaves nothing out of the stories, which touch on everything from *brujerías* (witchcraft) to *borracheras* (drunken sprees). With a simple eloquence, he relates how life on the ranch was difficult and often dangerous, but never lonely. A sense of community pervades all of Don Nasario's memories, from the cleaning of the *cequias* (ditches) to the *cosecha* (harvest).

Though these reminiscences might be considered "slices of life," they take on a larger, almost mythic dimension as we read them from the increasing distance of the twenty-first century. Part of the beauty and poignancy of this book derives from Don Nasario's own awareness of that "distance," as he speaks to us of a time when there was faith, respect, and unity of the people.

"Más antes había crianza"—"In the old days, there was respect," Don Nasario tells us. And the fields—why, compared to today, the crops they used to raise were amazing—"¡Allá se daban unas siembras que déjate!"

I couldn't help but remember my own father as I read these pages—my *suegro* who was truly a father to me. Like Nasario, I learned the life of a *ranchero* at my *suegro's* side—how to ride a horse, plow a field, and mix mud for the adobes to build our home.

But as Nasario reveals in these pages, the most important learning was embodied in the stories our fathers told

us as they taught us how to work. What they were doing was passing down a philosophy, a code of ethics, a way of life in those stories and reminiscences.

Listen, then, with Nasario, as his tata speaks to us of his life and ours.

Jim Sagel
Española, New Mexico

Introduction

Tata: A Voice from the Río Puerco is a collection of stories excerpted from interviews and informal conversations I have had over the last several years with my father, Nasario P. García. These exchanges date back to our first taped interview of 1979. Since then we have frequently discussed numerous topics related to his childhood, adolescence, and adult experiences in the Río Puerco valley, specifically in Guadalupe, where he spent most of his life before moving to Albuquerque in 1944.

Today he and former Río Puerco residents who are still physically able to travel visit the area from time to time. Some, such as Benjamín "Benny" Lucero and his wife Pina, from Cabezón, or Melaquías "Mel" Lovato, from San Luis, have even returned after retirement to the villages they once felt compelled to forsake. Others, in particular grandchildren or great-grandchildren who were not even born in the Río Puerco valley, are now trickling back with their sons and daughters to the villages of their parents, grandparents, or even great-grandparents. San Luis, the closest village to State Highway 44, is a good example. Ironically few grandchildren seem interested in restoring the old homes or building new ones; instead they are peppering their communities with mobile homes, a phenomenon (some say an eyesore) of the last several years in many rural Hispanic areas in New Mexico. These homes serve as retreats or "mountain cabins" on weekends away from the hustle and bustle of city life.

In its heyday, the Río Puerco valley comprised four active and thriving communities: Cabezón (La Posta), Casa Salazar, Guadalupe (Ojo del Padre), and San Luis, also known at one time as La Tijera (Map 1). Today they are all ghost towns, slowly melting into the earth whence

they once arose. Each has fallen victim to one set of circumstances or another, ranging from droughts and overgrazing to the drafting of young men during the World Wars. Such situations engendered an exodus from which the villages never recovered. One by one they fell—first Casa Salazar, then Cabezón, San Luis, and finally Guadalupe, in 1958.

The Río Puerco valley had two settlement periods. The first began in Navajo country in the 1760s, after the approval of several grazing grants by Governor Tomás Vélez Cachupín; the second occurred approximately one hundred years later, following the establishment of the Navajo Reservation. Around the 1860s and 1870s, settlers started to return to Casa Salazar, Cabezón, Guadalupe, and San Luis. People migrated to the Río Puerco valley from places like Albuquerque, Bernalillo, Alameda, Los Ranchos de Albuquerque, and Atrisco. Others came from as far away as Antón Chico, on the Río Pecos, southeast of Las Vegas. What motivated these people to venture westward to the Río Puerco valley is unclear, except that some left the Río Grande valley in the eighteenth and nineteenth centuries in search of a better living; others, curiously enough, were beginning to feel crowded in Albuquerque. This infusion of people resulted in Hispanic settlements that were to last until the late 1950s.

My paternal grandfather, Teodoro José García, was one of the original settlers in the second settlement wave, and also one of the last to leave in the 1950s. He was born in Algodones in 1872 and moved to Casa Salazar with his parents around 1880. His father, named Juan García, was blind and could not fend for himself and his family, so he depended on his wife Juliana and my grandfather for support. My grandfather also had a sister Paula

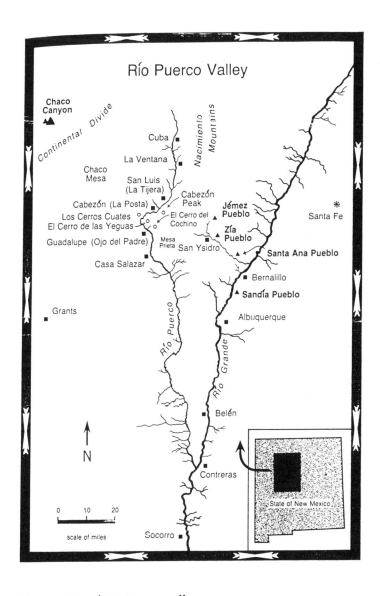

Map 1. Map of Río Puerco valley

and a younger brother Ramón, both of whom migrated to the Río Puerco valley with the family.

Around 1886–88, at fourteen or sixteen years of age, my grandfather was earning fifteen dollars per month as a cow wrangler for John Miller, a cattle rancher in Casa Salazar who also owned a country store. Half of the salary he earned monthly went for the groceries his mother charged at Miller's store. He kept the remaining $7.50. After John Miller died, my grandfather worked for the son, José Miller, who later entered politics and went to Bernalillo where he opened a bar, but he later went broke. In his relationship with the Millers, which lasted ten to fifteen years, my grandfather took care of herds of cattle numbering in the hundreds.

It was his association with the Millers that enabled him to save a few dollars before marrying my grandmother, Emilia Padilla García from Pecos, on December 10, 1898. She had gone from Pecos via Corrales as an orphan with family members to Casa Salazar in the 1890s, after her father was killed on the railroad. Both were evidently quite poor at the time of their marriage. According to an aunt of mine, Teodorita García-Ruelas, their home after the wedding was a corral turned bedroom with virtually nothing but blankets for a mattress and some personal effects. Thereafter he continued working for the Miller family, taking care of his blind father until the latter died in 1899 or 1900, a few years after his mother passed away.

About this time my grandparents purchased their first piece of property in el Rincón del Cochino, along the Río Puerco not far from la Placita de Guadalupe (see figure 1). The land consisted of a strip fifty yards by half a mile long, where they built a house, farmed, raised animals, and began to have a family. Thanks to her ingenuity and

his hard work, they prospered, purchasing properties in Guadalupe, twice in 1918 and again in 1931. They had already acquired a home in Martíneztown in Albuquerque in 1912.

By 1918 my grandfather was a freighter for Richard (Ricardo) Heller, who was a merchant and rancher in Cabezón. He hauled foodstuffs and other provisions from Albuquerque for Heller's Trading Post. My grandparents were effusive in crediting him for their success, because it was he who, through the *partido* system, helped them build up their own livestock holdings, principally cattle, that led to their self-sufficiency. At one time (around 1928), they owned at least one hundred cattle, dozens of

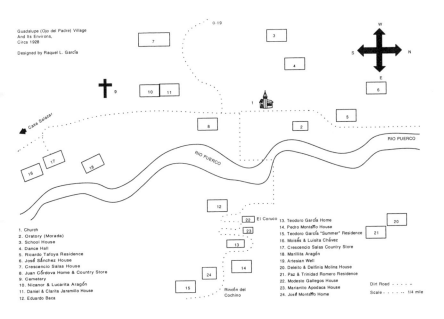

Figure 1. Guadalupe (Ojo del Padre) village and its environs, c. 1928. Designed by Raquel L. García.

horses, countless goats and hogs, plus luscious fields of corn, wheat, and pinto beans. Poor people would even frequent their home for a free meal during taxing times. These kinds of gestures were no doubt instrumental in keeping close-knit families and communities in the Río Puerco from disintegrating.

According to the 1880 census, Casa Salazar, Cabezón, Guadalupe, and San Luis, were all well established by then. Casa Salazar claimed 200 inhabitants; Guadalupe, where I grew up, numbered 161 inhabitants; San Luis had 97 people; and Cabezón's population, since it was not enumerated separately, is unclear.

The 1910 census shows that Casa Salazar and Guadalupe combined numbered 357 people, compared to 361 in 1880, when they were listed separately; therefore their respective populations seem to have held steady. The same assumption can be drawn with regard to Cabezón and San Luis. Although La Ventana, south of Cuba, was included with Cabezón and San Luis in the 1910 census, their combined populations numbered 359. Thus one can reasonably assume that Cabezón's and San Luis's populations also remained basically unchanged between 1880 and 1910.

It was not until World War I and thereafter that people such as my father began to leave the Río Puerco valley for good, because of scarcity of water, insufficient crops, and other disrupting factors. Among these latter influences, albeit somewhat insignificant due to their very small number, were young men who refused to return to ranching and farming following their tour of duty after World War I. Also at least one family, according to my father, abandoned Guadalupe around 1928, since the husband was able to procure employment with the Santa Fe

Railroad shops in Albuquerque. But the exodus of people from the Río Puerco valley began in earnest in the 1930s. The reasons varied.

First came the fencing of the *mercedes*, or land grants (around 1932), in particular the Ojo del Espíritu Santo Grant, where most ranchers from Guadalupe, Cabezón, and San Luis had pastured their cattle on the free lands. The U.S. government imposed land-restriction policies (such as the Taylor Grazing Act, in 1934); in order to ensure adherence to these policies, federal rangers (*rinches*) were dispatched to the Río Puerco valley to remove all livestock from the Ojo del Espíritu Santo Grant. This evoked immense resentment and hostility against government officials, because numerous ranchers found themselves in possession of more animals than they had land or water to support. "The government was very unfair to us" ("El gobierno jue muy ingrato con nosotros"), said my grandfather. To add insult to injury, "The rich men," both Anglos and Hispanics, "rented the best lands, the best pastures" ("Los hombres ricos arrentaron los mejores terrenos, los mejores pasteos"), also a contributing factor to the demise of villages like Guadalupe.

To compound the dilemma, a terrible drought hit the Río Puerco valley in the mid-1930s. In some cases more than half of the ranchers' cattle perished. Crops did not fare any better. To avoid the further starvation of livestock, the government stepped in to assist ranchers and farmers. Each rancher was given from one to two tons of hay per month to feed his animals, while every family received a flat grant of twenty-five dollars per month to purchase food. The assistance continued for a year or so, until the drought passed and people were able to regain some economic stability.

A final but decisive blow was the rupturing of a reservoir dam north of the village that had provided water for farms as far south as Casa Salazar (Map 1). This happened around 1937 or 1938 and broke people's spirits. The government's refusal to help rebuild the dam further disillusioned most of them to the point of giving up farming, since they could no longer divert water into the *acequia* system for irrigating their crops. Government officials apparently found the cost of reconstructing the dam exorbitant.

The end result for the villagers was a blunted double-edged sword. Their livelihood, which stemmed from raising cattle both for commercial and domestic purposes and from crops such as corn, wheat, and pinto beans, which were often sold or traded, suddenly was threatened. Those families who did attempt to eke out an existence were at the mercy of mother nature in an arid environment. People's spirits continued to fall. But they were hearty individuals with unlimited religious faith, and so some endured until they could no longer depend on their land or their cattle for sustenance.

Their hopes fading and the future darkened, the last remaining people boarded up their homes for good in the 1950s and headed for Albuquerque and other surrounding communities, in the hope of improving their lot elsewhere.

My father was the youngest of three brothers and three sisters and spent many years in Guadalupe, but in 1944 he was forced, like so many other *rancheros* before and after him, to abandon ranch life in search of a better living in Albuquerque. His first job (1944–45) in Albuquerque was with the Wool Warehouse Company. He worked for forty to forty-five cents per hour, stacking cowhides and sorting the wool brought in from ranches in rural New Mexico. After a year he was laid off, so he went to work

for Crane O'Fallon Company, at 612 North First Street, a plumbing fixtures wholesale distributor. When he began working for this company he earned sixty-five cents per hour. Within eight or ten years he was promoted to warehouse manager (not bad for someone with a fifth-grade education), a position he held until his retirement in 1974. By then his wages had risen to around four dollars per hour; his retirement benefits would not be much better.

But, my father's tenure with Crane O'Fallon Company served as a rude and instructive awakening to both of us. He often said to me, "Get an education so you can get an office job like Mr. Smith," his supervisor. Thanks to his foresight and insistence, I followed his advice. Today my father only has a vague notion of my career as an educator, but he takes heart in my having heeded his advice. What more could one ask for?

Following our move to Albuquerque, my father continued to visit Guadalupe (my mother and my brothers and sisters and I spent several summers there) and still does today. He has sold all of his cattle and his grazing permit but has retained his property. Since the death of his parents in 1972, however, and because of the subsequent settling of their estate, he no longer owns the house he and my mother built, shortly after they were married in 1935.

My mother, Agapita López-García, born in San Miguel, about nine miles southeast of Cuba, and my father spent nine memorable but difficult years in Guadalupe—from 1935 to 1944. After moving to Albuquerque, we lived in Martíneztown for the next four years (1944–48); the rest of the time we lived in Los Ranchos de Albuquerque, where we built a home and where my father has lived alone, since my mother passed away in 1972.

The stories in this book span the years from 1917 to 1944. They are reminiscent of the *cuadros de costumbres*, realistic descriptions or scenes of daily activities, customs, and manners, that flourished in early nineteenth-century Spain. The *cuadros*, like my father's stories, are regional in scope and consist of short, individual story frameworks populated with real people, places, and animals; they bring to light local life in a picturesque and oftentimes less than glamorous way.

As we read my father's accounts, we should reflect on the fact that he never went beyond the fifth grade. This does not detract from his innate intelligence, however; he is bright and perceptive, with an assured sense of purpose and being. To this day, at age eighty-two, he has an uncanny ability to recall even the most minute detail, however insignificant it may seem. And when he cannot remember something, he will simply tell you very matter-of-factly, without apologies or any hint of embarrassment. That is my father: straightforward, incredibly honest, fair, and unwavering in his moral principles. He has always been, in the truest sense, *hombre de su palabra*, a man of his word.

He was a model of the foregoing qualities for us children, especially of respect for people. He had a saying: "No andes con las medias caidas ("Don't run around with your socks down to your ankles"). This was his way of telling us "to get our act together," never to be late for anything, especially mass. To do so was looked upon as disrespectful. My father also had his favorite *dicho*, or proverb, indelible in my mind to this day, and pronounced many times over the dinner table: "No hay mal que por bien no venga" ("Every cloud has a silver lining"). Today he still holds allegiance to this precept, because he always felt—and no doubt always will—that the embers of hope

and optimism are an integral part of our psyche and indispensable for survival on this earth, regardless of the circumstances that surround or confront us.

Being the oldest of eight children, I was taught the art of independence, responsibility, and self-discipline. Hence I enjoyed the enviable role of feeling important at a tender age, because many responsibilities fell on my shoulders. In my father's absence, for example, I strived to fill his shoes as far as ranch chores were concerned. These included chopping wood, feeding the chickens and cows, hoeing, and generally assisting my mother. She and I spent a lot of time alone when I was small, while my father was away at work during the week building roads and repairing water channels under the auspices of the WPA. The tender relationship between my mother and me grew and became very special.

But the relationship with my dad, *tata* (a term of endearment), was, in retrospect, also special. I attribute this in large measure to my being the first child. As a result he spoiled me by bringing home from work on weekends small brown bags full of hard candy, which I consumed in short order. Later I was to suffer the consequences, with my share of cavities and toothaches, much to my chagrin, since dentists were unheard of out on the ranches.

Once my father returned to the ranch full-time, our relationship grew stronger as I got older. In the process I learned numerous things from him, some by observation, others through instruction. He taught me how to ride a horse, plow the soil, rope calves, raise rabbits, and use a scythe, a hammer, and a saw.

Through all these activities, my father conveyed his own work ethic as he knew and perceived it. He used to say: "Haz las cosas al revés, y las haces otra vez," the equivalent of "Haste makes waste." But the idea went

beyond this mere suggestion; it was an admonishment to do the best job possible the first time. Anything short of this expectation was deemed sloppy and not to his satisfaction.

This philosophy and other aspects of my father's life emerge throughout these stories, but more importantly, his recollections speak to us from a vanished time, as expressed many, many years later in the voice of a man looking back across time and space, to recount his experiences in a sincere and lucid manner. The voice of today is not the voice of long ago, but somehow they both meet, coalesce, and crystallize, to bring forth a past laden with pleasant—and not so pleasant—memories. Yesterday's voice is impressionable, crisp, and vibrant; today's is nostalgic, reflective, and somber. But when they come together, their unmistakable beauty and resonance illuminate and enliven a past that should not be forgotten, a past not only of life on the farm or ranch, but also a manifestation of a way of life that will finally cease to exist when voices like my father's become silent. The eminent Spanish philosopher Miguel de Unamuno (1864–1936) once said: "the truth [lies] in life and life [lies] in truth." That is the spirit embodied in this book.

It is my father's story, then and now, as he describes candidly and unabashedly his experiences on the ranch. As he reflected on a faraway past, he repeatedly employed the expression "En ese tiempo," "back then, in those days," as if to punctuate the memories of yesteryear. These reminiscences evince a pastoral existence that today is anachronistic and somewhat blurred for most of us. What we can visualize and grasp in reading my father's accounts is the people's indefatigable spirit and ability to survive. This was perhaps the single most important trait of the inhabitants of the Río Puerco valley, a beautiful yet harsh

and unforgiving land, where rattlesnakes, prairie dogs (*tuzas*) and some coyotes and lobos are the only fauna that still thrives today, long after the human families, compadres, comadres, primos, and other companions bade farewell to their beloved valley. But different species of birds, such as hawks (*gavilanes*) owls (*tecolotes*), and crows are much less visible today, having also faded into the past.

The format of this book is simple and straightforward. The stories appear in Spanish, with English translations. For those who know Spanish, regardless of whether they are New Mexico natives or not, the language will be found to be as pure and unadulterated as can be imagined, considering the fact that Spanish has existed in our state for over 450 years. True there is an occasional Anglicism (such as *troca* for "truck," but by and large, the Spanish my father uses is as Castillian (*castizo* as can be found anywhere in rural Spain (I can personally attest to this, having lived, studied, and traveled in Andalucía for almost a year and a half during my first visit to Spain. Several return trips have taken me to other parts of this Iberian country where the Spanish we have enjoyed for centuries in New Mexico was born).

In transcribing the stories that follow, I have left the language of the people, my father's dialect, virtually intact. Only in rare cases involving pronunciation, such as a *b* pronounced like a *v* (*estava* for *estaba*), was standard, modern orthography used. Also in most instances where linkages occurred (for instance *desto* for *de esto*), the latter was adopted in the transcription. Aside from these kinds of situations, the dialect in this collection is authentically that of my father. *Loo* (*luego*), *ansina* (*así*), *pus* or *pos* (*pues*), *teníanos* (*teníamos*), and countless other examples of archaic and/or regional Spanish, tenacious

survivals in the speech of a tenacious people, are found in the ensuing narratives.

A glossary juxtaposing regional words with the modern or standard versions is provided for the benefit of the student of Spanish. In this way one can see and appreciate the degree to which people of the Río Puerco valley maintained some words in their archaic or traditional form, while others were altered or new ones invented to accommodate and elaborate local linguistic fashion.

Tata
A Voice from the Río Puerco

I
A Wealth of Experiences, 1917–1922

Probably no individual is capable of probing the past to truly bring to life an intact childhood. Those of us who undergo any soul searching—and most of us do—are able at least to reconstruct bits and pieces of the remote past. It could be because those episodes command a special importance in our lives, and hence we are able to give life and spirit to them when called upon to do so. The importance of our early environment may well lie in our ability to bring to the fore both pleasant and unpleasant recollections. Rarely do people remember the myriad routine and emotionally neutral aspects of our daily lives.

That is the case with my father and people like him, who once resided in the Río Puerco valley. The environment in which he was reared as a child in Guadalupe made a tremendous impression on his own outlook on life. To this day he can still recreate his childhood world replete with joy and pleasure with the freshness typical of someone who, despite adversity, enjoyed his formative years in a rural setting of innocence, vitality, and isolation.

It is always easier—and often more exciting—to accentuate the positive; but undesirable experiences are not readily forgotten either, and they are therefore more apt to be remembered in spite of the pain in recreating them. We learn from both the negative and the positive; that is why old-timers are sometimes better able to depict early periods of their lives than, let us say, middle age. Our childhoods are much more formative and consequently easier to reconstruct, unfettered by all the careless or haphazard trappings of adolescence, the suspicion and cynicism of adulthood.

In this part my father takes us into his childhood world of the 1910s and 1920s (1917–22) in Guadalupe. He was born in Rincón del Cochino, not far from La Placita of

Guadalupe (see figure 1), in 1912, the year New Mexico became a state. He was the youngest of three brothers and three sisters, although two of his sisters, Petrita and Julianita, died of unknown illnesses while they were still very young. At the present time, he and his oldest brother, Ramón García, who is ninety years old, are the only surviving members of his family.

At the turn of the century, New Mexico was still struggling to achieve statehood after several fruitless attempts in the 1850s, 1860s, and 1870s. An effort was even launched to merge Arizona and New Mexico, but it died in 1906. When New Mexico finally became a state, on January 6, 1912, under President William Howard Taft, our constitution reflected a conservative political ideology that prevails even to this day among politicians and voters alike, regardless of political affiliation or ethnic identification.

Nevertheless when it came to World War I, irrespective of political party, New Mexico's patriotism made itself manifest by the thousands of young GIs who served their country abroad; the number drafted from the Río Puerco valley, and in particular from Guadalupe where my father resided, was apparently quite small, based on my interviews. Some returned to the Río Puerco following the war; others did not. Evidently few died in the war.

Of those who returned safely, an overwhelming number refused to return to farm life. The ones who did joined forces with their parents and grandparents to wrestle with problems that ranged from droughts to having little if any money for buying household goods and clothing. When the Great Depression struck in 1929, however, Río Puerco valley residents were in better shape economically, because by then the droughts were temporarily over, so farmers and ranchers could now live off the land and from

their livestock. To put it in a different perspective, they were able to put food on the table, often an impossible task for city dwellers.

Whatever problems or joys existed for families like my father's, they tended to be local in scope, although some, such as the influenza epidemic of the 1910s, were more universal. My father's story about "Inflencia" from when he was five or six years old, not only focuses on becoming paralyzed, but dramatizes the fact that many families were literally wiped out by the epidemic. But hardships at an early age were not limited to health problems per se. A case in point is the story on "La escuela" ("School"). Here we learn of children trudging for miles through snow in the winter to get to school, since there were no school buses, and because some parents did indeed want their sons and daughters to get educated.

The school year in Guadalupe usually lasted nine months, beginning in September and ending in May, but many children, boys in particular, missed school in the fall, at harvest season, or in the spring, when they helped their parents plant the fields. Even during the academic year, attendance seems to have been a hit-or-miss affair at best, due, for instance, to some parents' casual attitude toward education or because of health problems.

Most students only completed the second or third grade before quitting. Very few finished the eighth grade, which was the highest level of education they could obtain. Girls, for the most part, fared worse, because some were not even allowed to start school, let alone seek an education. In that respect parents (mostly fathers) assumed a rather cavalier attitude in adhering to and perpetuating the precept that the "woman's place was in the home."

The quality of schooling, from all indications, seems

to have ranged from fair to mediocre. English, for example, was the language of instruction, but, according to my father, Spanish prevailed for communication between students in the classroom and on the playgrounds, so they learned little English. A detriment to learning also was the fact that the majority of the teachers were young, mostly women from eighteen to twenty-one years of age, with only a high-school diploma in hand and hardly versed in pedagogy. The rare male teacher, whenever one could be contracted to teach, was no better prepared. Discipline in the classroom was never a problem, however.

When my father started first grade in Guadalupe, in 1918 or 1919, the enrollment was only ten or twelve students. The schoolhouse at that time was in La Placita, across the Río Puerco, some two to three miles from where he lived (see figure 1). He and his older sisters, Petrita and Julianita, were driven in a carriage (*bogue*) by their father. At times he was unable to take them, so they had to walk, regardless of the season, irrespective of weather conditions. At one time my father even rode a burro to school, feeding and watering it at recess time.

Respite from school for those who were conscientious in attending came in the summer, but the responsibilities for a nine or ten year old on the farm were awesome, if enjoyable, as we learn in "Yo cuidaba un atajo de cabras" ("I Took Care of a Herd of Goats"). But hard work alone sometimes was not enough; good fortune played a vital role as well. We learn of this in "Don Ricardo Heller," because it was he who helped my grandfather achieve self-sufficiency.

There existed also a kind of universal camaraderie and altruism among the villagers, whereby everyone "pitched in" and helped one another, as witnessed in "Él jue criando

vacas y sembraba" (He Started Raising Cattle and Farming") or "Limpiando la cequia" ("Cleaning the Ditch"). Some ranchers, such as my paternal grandfather, for example, were well-off ("En papá estaba muy bien") in comparison to others. Nevertheless even he was willing to help his fellow ranchers by hiring them as farmhands ("Los piones") in exchange for hay, corn, and other crops. Other farmers who were not busy year-round like my grandfather, augmented what little income they may have gained from farming by trapping during the winter months, as we see in "Ponían trampas" ("They'd Set Traps").

While people worked hard at earning a living, they also enjoyed themselves enthusiastically. We learn of outstanding dancers such as the "elder statesman," Don Modesto Gallegos, whom I heard of as a small boy. Such men had a good time without getting drunk, even though liquor was available. In "Mula" ("Corn Liquor"), we are taken into the private world of a bootlegger, an episode in my father's repertoire of childhood memories that remains especially vivid in his mind after all these years.

What comes across clearly in these vignettes of childhood is that life for a child like my father during the first two decades of this century was hardly an endearing experience by today's standards. Children, for example, rarely could play together, unless families visited each other on Sundays after mass, because people resided so far from one another. The closest neighbors sometimes lived up to four miles away except for those living in La Placita proper, where homes were closer to each other. It was a childhood of isolation; my father never talks about playing with other children his own age. His playmates were the goats, pigs, chickens, and household pets. At the same time, however, he was exposed to a variety of experiences,

some vicarious, others immediate, virtually all of them linked to his father, to whom he was close for over half a century, until he died at one hundred years of age in 1972.

18 DE OCTUBRE DE 1979
La inflencia

Yo me acuerdo, no muy bien, pero reclamaban, a lo que me platicaba en papá [Teodoro García], cuando la inflencia . . . porque yo cuando la inflencia, yo, yo me tullí. Y no podía caminar. Me acuerdo yo que, no sé con qué me curaría, antonces jue cuando la guerra. Y yo me acuerdo, estaba muy chiquito. Antonces vivíanos ai en la casa que es de Antonio ora. Abajo de la loma. Toavía no tenían lotra. Y me ponía mamá aá en una, me paraba en una camalta, y loo de aá me hacía correr a donde estaba lotra, pa que comenzara andar. Pero reclamaban, mi papá y mamá me platicaban que cuando, cuando la inflencia, que pegó muy juerte. Y es que había veces que muncha gente murió y que había munchas casas que quedaron vacías. Es que se moría toda la gente. Sí. Y algotros no. Conforme les juera tocando.

OCTOBER 18, 1979
Influenza

I remember, not very well, but people claimed, according to what Dad [Teodoro García] used to tell me, during the time of the influenza . . . because during the time of the influenza, I, I became crippled. And I couldn't walk. I remember that, I don't know what they cured me with, that was during the war [World War I]. And I recall, I was very small [five or six years old]. We were living at the time there in that house that now belongs to Antonio. Down the hill. They still didn't have the other one. And Mom used to put me on a, she'd put me next to a bed, and from there she would make me run to the other bed, so that I could begin to walk. But she claimed, my dad and mom would tell me that when, at the time of the influenza, that it hit very hard. And I understand that there were times when many people died and many homes were left without any people. I understand all the people would die. Yes. And others were more fortunate, according to their own fate.

School Children of Guadalupe (Rincón del Cochino), c. 1942.

18 DE OCTUBRE DE 1979
La escuela

Pues, sí, todos los que estaban allá [en Guadalupe]
despachaban a sus hijos a la escuela. Pero en ese
tiempo, en ese tiempo tenían que caminar a la escuela.
Posible algunos los traiban sus papases y algotros
tenían que ir [a pie]; o se cambiaban cerca, y otros
tenían que caminar dos o tres millas, pa ir a la escuela
a pie.

Pues, eh, íbanos yo, Teodora, y Julianita, y hasta
Petra [sus hermanas], pienso. Yo estaba muy chiquito.
¡A pie, no te digo! Llevábanos lonche. Y cuando caiba

OCTOBER 18, 1979
School

Well, yes, everyone who was over in Guadalupe sent
their children to school. But back then, in those days
they had to walk to school. Perhaps for some of them
their parents took them and others had to walk; or
some moved closer to school; and others had to walk
two or three miles, to get to school.

Well, ah, Teodora, Julianita, and even Petra [his
sisters] and I went, I believe. I was very small. I'm
telling you, on foot! [It would take about forty-five
minutes.] We would take lunch. And whenever it

nieve, que caiba nieve entre el día, en papá iba a
toparnos en un bogue pa trainos.

No había chopos. Too lo que usábanos de chopos era
guangoches. Pos, allá [en la escuela] nos quitábanos los
guangoches. Pero y nomás iba uno a pisar la nieve y se
engolvía uno los chopos. Ya sabía uno cómo
doblárselos, *muy bien*. Y luego agarraba uno alambre de
este de tercio y se los amarraba aquí, loo pacá.

Oh, en papá ésa era una cosa que a él no le gustaba,
que faltara uno de la escuela. Y al último no, ya al
último pusieron escuela pa este otro lao [del río]. Y loo
ya después, pos esto jue ora al último [de los treinta en
adelante], ya antonces sí estaba moderno. Tenían
school bus [la Placita] y too.

Pues, eh, yo no estoy seguro si cuando estuve allá en
Gualupe, pienso que allá comenzó [a enseñar] en prima
Toñita [Leyba]. Y luego cuando pusieron la escuela
aquí [de este lado del río] estuvo un tiempo en prima
Toñita y luego no me acuerdo cómo se llama, la
Mague, no me acuerdo cómo se llama. El cuento es que
. . . yo iba en un burro. Y la mestra se retrató conmigo;
estoy parao y ella subida en el burro. En primo Liverato
[Leyba] me enseñó el retrato. ¡Fíjate tú cuántos años
hace! Y en primo Liverato y en prima Toñita tienen el
retrato ese . . .

Cuando ya se llegaban las nueve, pus salía la mestra
y sonaba una campanita, y le liniaba a uno. Y loo de ai
tenía uno que entrar en línea, y cada quien a su banco.
Cada uno estaba solo en su banco. Todos [juntos].
Todos. No era más de un cuarto.

Pos, yo estaba muy chiquito cuando estuve aá.
Cuando yo estaba poquito más grande es cuando
cambiaron la escuela pacá [de este lado del río]. Y loo
ya después no, ya depués me vine pacá pa la Plaza. En

snowed, when it snowed during the day, Dad would go meet us in a horse buggy to bring us back.

There weren't any overshoes. What we used for overshoes was burlap. Well, at school we'd take off the burlap. As soon as you were to step out in the snow, you'd wrap up your shoes with burlap. We already knew how to wrap the burlap *quite well* around the shoes. And then you grabbed bailing wire and stitched it here and there.

Oh, that was one thing Dad didn't like, for us to miss school. Toward the end, later on they set up school on this side [of the river]. And then afterwards, this was much later [from the 1930s onward], things were much more modern. They had a school bus and all [instead of a covered wagon heated by a pot-bellied stove].

Well, ah, I'm not sure if it's when I was over in Guadalupe [la Placita], I believe that's when prima Toñita [Leyba] started teaching. And then when they moved the school to this side of the river, prima Toñita was there for a while and then I don't know what her name is, Mague (Maggie), I believe, I don't remember her name. The fact is that . . . I used to go to school on a donkey. And the teacher took her picture with me in it; I'm standing and she's on the donkey. Primo [cousin] Liverato Leyba showed me the picture. Just imagine how many years ago that was! And primo Liverato and prima Toñita have that picture . . .

When nine o'clock came around, well, the teacher would come out and ring the little bell, and she'd line you up. From there you had to enter lined up in a row, and everyone to their desks. Everyone was alone at their desk. We were all together. All of us. It was only one room.

Martínez [Town]. Oh, yo creo que cuando vine aquí comencé en el libro tercero, pienso. [Con] la, la Matthew. ¡Y qué mestra tan mala! ¡Chiva! Coja, *pero mala*. Uh, muy mala.

Well, I was very small when I was over on the other side of the river. When I was a little older is when they moved the school to this side of the river. Later on, no, afterward I came here to Albuquerque. In Martínez Town. Oh, I believe that when I came here I was in the third grade [about 1921, Santa Barbara School]. With Mrs., Mrs. Matthew. Boy, what a mean teacher! Mean! Lame, *but mean*. Wow, very mean!

Nasario P. García herding goats, c. 1920. Courtesy of Teodorita García-Ruelas.

18 DE OCTUBRE DE 1979
Yo cuidaba un atajo de cabras

En ese tiempo, en ese tiempo se costumbraba que la gente tenía dos o tres vacas de leche. Ya cada quien sabía. En la tarde tenía que ir a corretiar las vacas, encerrar el becerro, pa ordeñar las vacas otro día en la mañana. Cada quien asegún le tocaba.

Por ejemplo, por ejemplo, como ora yo cuando estaba mediano, yo cuidaba un atajo de cabras. Ése era el oficio mío. Papá tenía, oh, como ochenta, cien cabras. En un burro, en un burro. No con sillas de esas, en una silla burrera, en un burro. Me iba en de la mañana y ai

OCTOBER 18, 1979
I Used to Take Care of a Herd of Goats

Back then, back then it was customary for people to have two or three dairy cows. Everyone knew his chores. In the afternoon you had to go after the cows, lock up the calf, so as to milk the cows the next morning. Everyone tended to his chores.

For example, for example, like me when I was small, I took care of a herd of goats. That was my responsibility. Dad had, oh, about eighty, one hundred goats. On a donkey, on a donkey. Not with one of those regular saddles, on a donkey saddle, on a donkey. I'd take off very early in the morning and there I was

me andaba cuidando las cabras. ¡Uh! Yo tendría como ocho, diez años.

En el verano eso era todo lo que hacía. Pus yo estaba mediano. Pues allá me iba; me acuerdo que me iba cuidar las cabras y luego en papá me hacía una jonda. Ai me andaba cazando. Había veces que cazaba conejos y los, cómo, los desollaba y los asaba.

Había veces que pa medio día venía, encerraba las cabras en el corral, como ora en el verano que es los días largos, comía, descansaba y loo nomás resfrescaba, y les daba a las cabras otra vez.

taking care of the goats. Boy! I must have been about eight, ten years old [1920–22].

In the summer that's all I did. Understand that I was small. There I went; I remember I'd go take care of the goats and then my dad would make me a slingshot. I'd spend my time hunting. There were times when I'd shoot rabbits and I'd, how do you say, I'd dress them and roast them.

There were times that by noon I'd return home, lock up the goats in the corral, like now during the summer when the days are long, eat, rest, and as soon as it was cool, I'd take the goats out again.

18 DE OCTUBRE DE 1979
Mula

En tiempos pasaos no había cantinas en Gualupe, pero hacían mula. Y de ai era onde se emborrachaban. Pero antonces no había hombres o personas que jueran alcojólicos. Cuando tocaba que hacían bailes, se embolaban; sí, pero pasó, pasó. No había peleas. Uh, una que otra vez, ai en vez en cuando, pos, iban y compraban según lo que les gustaba, y se emborrachaban y se daban moquetes.

Pues yo te voy a decir. ¡Fíjate tú! Yo tendría como diez años. El primero que yo conocí que comenzó hacer mula jue el dijunto Todosio Montaño. De allá dionde tenía la casa Pedro Montaño, pallá pal rumbo del Cañoncito. Ai vivía él. Él jue el primero que yo vide que comenzó hacer mula, pero conocí poquito de eso.

Después cuando ya se vinieron los Montaños pacá pa Albuquerque, muncho despúes, había otro hombre, no me acuerdo de su nombre, que conocía a estos Montaños. Ai en el Cañoncito, en ese rincón, ai está una loma, y pal lao del rincón de esta loma, ai juquiaron, y hicieron cuartito tan grande como esta cocina el hombre este y sus compañeros. Ai mero hacían mula porque estaban escondidos.

Al último ya pa salirse la gente de la placita de Gualupe, el que hacía mula era el dijunto Paz Romero, el que crió a Adriano. Porque el dijunto este, Paz Romero, . . . yo no sé si mi padrino Leonardo y mi madrina Eloisa, lo llevaron a Adriano al rancho de medianito. Ai se crió él, con el dijunto Paz.

Tú sabes una botellita de esas de *Coca-Cola*, no de

OCTOBER 18, 1979
Corn Liquor

Back in the old days, there were no bars in Guadalupe,
but they made corn liquor. And that's what they got
drunk on. But long ago, there were no men or anybody
else who might be alcoholics. Whenever there was a
dance, they got drunk, yes, but it'd come and go. There
were no fights. Oh, once in a while there was one here
or there; well, they'd go and buy whatever they liked,
get drunk, and get into fistfights.

Well, I'll tell you. Imagine! I must have been about
ten years old. The first person I knew who started to
make corn liquor was the late Todosio Montaño. From
over there where Pedro Montaño had his house, in the
direction of el Cañoncito (the Little Canyon). That's
where he lived. He's the first one I saw who started to
make corn liquor, but just the same I learned very little
about that business.

Afterward, when the Montaños moved to
Albuquerque, long after, there was another man, I don't
remember his name, who knew the Montaños. There
in el Cañoncito, in that corner, there's a hill, and to
one side of the hill, that's where they dug out a trench
and made a small room as big as this kitchen, this man
and his buddies. Right there is where they made corn
liquor, because they were hidden.

Later on, about the time people were ready to
abandon Guadalupe, the one who used to make corn
liquor was the late Paz Romero, the one who raised
Adriano. Because the late Paz Romero, . . . I don't know
whether it was my godfather Leonardo and my
godmother Eloisa as well, who took Adriano to the

las grandes; ora hay grandes. En ese tiempo había de esas chiquitas. Un peso. Pero con una botella de esas se emborrachaban como tres o cuatro. ¡Porque era lumbre!

Pero mira, el que sí tenía y hacía muncha, y güena mula, jue el dijunto Todosio y ese otro hombre que te digo yo, y don Paz. Echabas, echabas como ora ai en suelo, tirabas una poquita de mula, y le prendías un fósforo y se prendía como gaselín.

La mula la hacían de maiz. De maiz y no sé qué otra cosa le echarían, pero ése era lo que llegué a ver yo. Tenían unos de esos barriles de palo, enchorraos asina, jirviendo y luego le echaban no sé si pasas. Y cuando ya lo echaban en la estiladora, vaporizaba, y de ai salía en el vapor, de ai salía la mula.

Y pa dale color—tenían un frasco abajo onde caiba— tostaban uno de estos orejones de durazno, que quedaba, ¿cómo quiero decir? Tostao, y ai goteaba. Cuando caiba allá, agarraba color lo mesmo que el juisque. Asina le daban color. Buscaban un durazno grande, ves, lo tosaban bien, no quemao, y de ai estaba goteando la mula, y caindo a una demasana o lo que juera. Cuando caiba allá, pos estaba del color del juisque.

Porque yo llegué a ir con en papá cuando estaba el dijunto Todosio. Yo iba con en papá, ¿ves? Estaba chiquito. Yo entraba, y allí andaba con en papá porque pus era compadre de en papá el dijunto Todosio. Y yo via allí todo.

ranch [from Albuquerque] while he was still very small. That's where he grew up, with the late Paz.

You know what one of those small bottles of Coca-Cola looks like, not the big ones; now there are big ones. Back then, there were those little ones. One dollar. But three or four could get drunk on one of those bottles. Because it was fire!

But listen, the one who had and made a lot, and good corn liquor, was the late Todosio and that other man I told you about—and don Paz. You could pour, like now on the floor, a little bit of moonshine and light a match, and it'd burn like gasoline.

Moonshine was made from corn, and I don't know what else they'd throw in it, but that's what I managed to see. They had those wooden barrels, in a straight line like this, boiling, and then they'd toss in raisins or I don't know what. And by the time they put the corn in the still, it'd steam. Steam would come out. That's where the corn liquor came out.

And in order to give it some color—there was a jug below the barrel, where the liquor came out—they'd toast one of these dried peaches [halves]. Then it dripped. When it dripped, it took on the exact same color as whiskey. That's how they gave it color. They'd look for a large peach, you see, toast it well, not burnt, and there you had the liquor dripping into a large jug or whatever. When the liquor came out, it was the color of whiskey.

Because I got to go with my father when the late Todosio was still alive. I used to accompany my father, you see. I was very small. I'd go in and look around with him, since he ws a *compadre* of the late Todosio. And I'd see everything in there.

El dijunto
Modesto Gallegos

Pues, ai, el que era muy mentao, ya era hombre grande cuando yo lo conocí, el dijunto Modesto Gallegos. Eso jue cuando yo estaba muy chiquito. ¡Oh! El dijunto Modesto, era un hombre pa polquiar que déjate.

¡Oh! Ese hombre, y ya era hombre grande. El día de San Juan, el día de Santana, que corrían gallo, él se metía en medio junto con los muchachos. ¡Y ya era hombre grande! Y muy liviano, y güeno era. ¡Oh! Y le gustaba muncho tamién . . . Beber.

Ai, ése es, el que tenía la mula. Sí. Este don Modesto tenía, casi siempre andaba en una mula, y esa mula era muy ligera. Y había veces que cuando andaba a caballo como el día de San Juan, asina, usaba un caballo. Oh ése, se entreveraba ai con los más jóvenes. A echar carreras, a todo. Sí. Ora pa bailar, ¡que déjate! Ese hombre yo ai en Gualupe que yo viera, de la vida de ese hombre, de la vida y el ánimo que tenía ese hombre.

Sí, era, quizás, muy mañosa la mula. Y no lo dejaba subirse y tenía en veces que tapale los ojos pa subirse en ella (risas).

OCTOBER 18, 1979
The Late Modesto Gallegos

Well, over there, the one who had made a name for himself, he was already an old man when I knew him, was the late Modesto Gallegos. That's when I was very small. Oh! The late Modesto, he was a man that when it came to dancing polkas, there was no one like him.

Oh! That man, and he was already old, on Saint John's Day, on Saint Anne's Day, during rooster racing, he got in the middle, alongside the young studs. And he was an old man! And very quick, and he was good. Oh! And he liked very much to . . . drink.

He's the one who had the mule. Yes. This Don Modesto had, he almost always was riding a mule, and that mule was very quick. And there were times when he was on horseback; then he'd just use a horse. Oh that man, he'd intermingle with the rest of the young guys. In racing, in everything. Yes. Now for dancing, wow! From what I saw of that man there in Guadalupe, the life that man led, the life and spirit he had, he had no equal.

Yes, I understand that his mule was very tricky. And she wouldn't let him get on so at times he had to cover her eyes in order to get on (laughter).

Un perro golondrino

Éste era un perro golondrino. Bueno, tenía . . . era no negro, negro, como renegrido, y tenía aquí las manos y las patas como amarillosas.

Y este perro, pues estaba entrando este toro a la milpa. Era como en agosto, setiembre. Venía y brincaba el cerco. Y loo iba en papá con el perro y se lo troteaba. Este perro le siguía y se le emparejaba hasta que lo agarraba del hocico, ¡y lo tumbaba! Ese perro yo lo llegué a ver. Nomás levantaba la cabeza el toro, se apalancaba [el perro] pa bajo y lo tumbaba. Parecía que no, pero lo llegué a ver. Era [el perro] regular; pesaría como setenta libras, yo creo. Tenía manias; sabía.

A Brownish-Yellow Dog

It was a brownish-yellow dog. Well, it had . . . it wasn't black, black, like blackish, and had like yellowish paws and legs.

And this dog, why this bull kept coming into the cornfield; it was like in August, September. It'd come and jump the fence. Then Dad would go with the dog and he'd set the dog on the bull. This dog would follow it and face it head on until he'd grab him by the snout, and he'd knock him down! Yes! I got to see that dog do that. As soon as the bull lifted its head, the dog would brace itself downward and knock him down. It seemed incredible, but I got to see it. The dog was average size. I believe it weighed about seventy pounds. He had his tricks; he knew what to do.

18 DE OCTUBRE DE 1979
Él jue criando vacas y sembraba

Güeno, yo te voy a decir. En papá, yo estaba muy chiquito, chico, yo me acuerdo. En papá comenzó, pa comenzar él tenía, él fletiaba con dos tiros de caballos. El carro, ponían dos, tres umentos. Fletiaban pa Cuba y pa Alburquerque. Traiban flete y llevaban. Y asina jue como en papá comenzó.

Ya después cuando él dejó ese negocio, que ya tuvo el terreno, por ejemplo, que aplicó ese *homestead*, antonces él se metió, él jue criando, él jue criando vacas y sembraba. Ya último en papá tenía güen atajo de vacas y sembraba muncho él. Asina jue como hacía la vida él.

Y pa sembrar, en ese tiempo, no había motores; no había nada. Con, con araos de manceba, a pie. Tenía uno que andar, con tiros de caballo. Asina era como hacían la vida. Asina vivían, sí.

Pues, eh, casi, en general, la gente ha sido muy unida. En esos años la gente se ayudaba una con otra. Cuando en papá iba a sembrar, o el vecino lotro, se juntaban y se ayudaban unos a los otros. Y pa echar el maiz ocupaban una persona pa que juera echando el maiz. Pero se juntaban tres, cuatro, o cinco. Y cuando ya acababan, iban ayudale al otro, al otro vecino, a sembrar. Sí. Asina era como lo hacían.

Pa la escardaba, pa la escardada, por ejemplo, pus ai, si ya cuando la plebe comenzó ya a crecer, pus ai lo mesmo ayudaba la mujer que los hijos, que todos. Y con *cavador*, no, no con . . . a juerza de cavador. Tenían una, tenía una de estas escardaderas con un

OCTOBER 18, 1979
He Started Raising Cattle and Farming

Well, I'm going to tell you. My dad, I was very small, small, I remember. My dad got started, to begin with he had, he freighted [from Cabezón to Albuquerque] with two teams of horses. The wagon, they'd add two, three sideboards to it. They carried freight to Cuba and to Albuquerque. They'd bring freight back and forth. And that's how my dad got started.

Sometime afterwards, when he left that line of work, when he already had his land, for example, after he applied for "homestead," then he got into, he started raising, he started raising cattle and farming. Toward the end of his life Dad had a good herd of cattle and he planted a lot. That's how he made a living.

As for farming, back in those days, there were no motors; there wasn't anything like that. With, with old-fashioned plows, on foot. You had to walk, with a team of horses. That's how they made a living. That's how they earned a living, yes.

Well, ah, the people in general, almost always, were very united. Back in those days people helped one another. Whenever Dad or a neighbor was going to plant, everyone got together and helped one another. And to sow the corn a person was hired so that he could sow the corn. But three, four, or five would get together. And whenever they finished, they'd go help the other neighbor plant. Yes. That's how they did it.

During the hoeing season, during the hoeing season, for example, by the time the children started to grow up, why the wife, just as much as the children, helped.

caballo, que le daban por el medio. Y luego, los otros venían con los cavadores quitándole la yerba alrededor y arrimándole tierra a la mata. Y así se iban.

Everyone did. And with a *hoe*, not, not with . . . just the hoe. They had one, they had one of these weeders pulled by a horse, that they'd take down the middle on either side of the row of plants. And then, the others would follow with the hoes, removing the weeds around the plant and pushing dirt around it. And that's the way they did it.

Don Ricardo Heller

Me acuerdo, me acuerdo poco. Don Ricardo era un hombre de los que estaba rico. Ése era uno de los hombres ricos ai en el Cabezón. Ese hombre, tenía no sé qué tantos atajos de borregas. Y tenía vacas, no munchas, pero tenía y tenía tienda. Él compraba lana y vendía. Era hombre que negociaba y ocupaba a muncha gente pa que trabajara con él.

A mí me platicaba en papá que él trabajó muncho con don Ricardo y agarró vacas al partido de don Ricardo, y asina jue como puso vacas en papá. Yo creo que el dijunto Ricardo le había ayudao pa que en papá pusiera vacas. Porque en papá, güeno, los Romeros, y todos, todos, había munchos que tenían vacas, pero a en papá en ese tiempo, yo creo que en papá tendría de malas, cuando yo estaba muy chiquito, de malas, de malas, no se le caiba de, de doscientas, trescientas vacas.

¡Oh sí! En papá estaba bien. Oh, en papá tenía caballadas, setenta, ochenta caballos sin marca, y marcaos. ¡Déjate! Ora en papá tenía muy güen atajo de vacas. Ése era cuando yo estaba muy chiquito.

Pero en papá me platicaba que el dijunto Ricardo, y mamá, que tenía[n] que agradecele. Ellos querían muncho a don Ricardo, que don Ricardo había levantao a en papá, mira. Vacas, es que le dio al partido y lo levantó, creo. Y en papá jue muy inteligente. En papá, él no andaba durmiendo hasta mediodía. De la madrugada, ya él andaba, hasta la medianoche.

Don Ricardo Heller

I remember, I remember a little. Don Ricardo was one
of those men who was rich. He was one of the rich
men there in Cabezón. That man, had, I don't know
how many flocks of sheep. And he had cows, not
many, but he did, and he also had a store. He bought
and sold wool. He was a man who traded and hired a
lot of people so they'd work for him.

My dad used to tell me that he worked lots for Don
Ricardo, and he contracted for cows with Don Ricardo
on the partido system, and that's how Dad started
raising cattle. I believe that the late Don Ricardo
helped Dad so he could start raising cattle. Because
Dad, okay, the Romeros, and everybody else, everyone,
many of them had cattle, but Dad back in those days, I
believe must have had about, when I was little, about,
about, no fewer than, than, two hundred, three hundred
cows.

Oh, yes! Dad was well-off. Oh, Dad had herds of
horses, seventy, eighty unbranded horses, and branded.
No kidding. Now Dad also had a good herd of cattle.
That's when I was very small.

But Dad would tell me that he and Mom had to be
grateful to the late Don Ricardo. They liked Don
Ricardo very much because he had given Dad a helping
hand, you see. I understand he gave him cows on the
partido system and helped him get off the ground. And
Dad was very intelligent. Dad was not the type to be
sleeping late. From daybreak, he was already on the go,
till way into the night.

19 DE MARZO DE 1992
Al partido

Como ora en papá tenía, . . . pa que lo que me platicó él así comenzó él. Agarró vacas al partido del dijunto Ricardo [Heller]. Depende qué tantos animals agarrara, pero de *cada* cinco animales, tenía que dale uno al del partido. ¿Entiendes? En otras palabras, si eran veinte animales, tenía que dale cinco [cuatro] becerros al del partido. Cada año. De cada cinco, uno. Eso es al partido.

Y si iban al tercio, si agarraban veinte vacas, o lo que agarraran, no le entregaban al partido. Si agarraban veinte o veinte y cinco, güeno, dígase que jueran veinte y cinco, a los cincos años tenía que entregale cincuenta. Eso es al tercio.

El partido no. Uno [un becerro] de cada cinco vacas. Tuvieran becerros [las vacas] o no tuvieran . . . y al partido lo que tiene que si uno agarra . . . de la mesma edá que agarra uno los animales, tiene uno que entregar. Si agarra uno quince, esas quince tiene uno que entregárselas, de la mesma edá que las recibe. Y el partido cada año. De cada cinco vacas, un becerro. Naturalmente. Le estaba asegurando el principal. Al partido no le importa si se morían dos o tres. Cuando se llegaba el tiempo de recibir sus vacas tenía que recibir la mesma cantidá.

No sé con borregas; no sé con borregas. Fácil que sea lo mesmo; no sé. Pero de vacas sí sé yo.

The Partido System

Like now Dad, according to what he told me, that's how he got started. He got cows on the *partido* system with the late Ricardo [Heller]. Depending on how many animals he contracted for, but from *every* five, he had to give one in return to the head of the partido system. Do you understand? In other words, if there were twenty cows, one had to give five [*sic*] calves to the partido chief. Every year. Out of every five, one. That's how the partido system works.

And if you went with the *tercio* system, if you got twenty cows, or whatever, it didn't work like the partido system. If you got twenty or twenty-five cows, okay, let's say it was twenty-five, at the end of five years you had to return fifty. That's how the tercio system works.

Not so on the partido system. One out of every five cows, whether they had calves or not . . . and one thing about the partido is that if you participate in it . . . the age of the animals that you receive must be the same when you return them. If you get fifteen, those fifteen must be of the same age when you return them. And in the partido system you do this once a year. From every five cows, a calf. Of course you have to guarantee the head of the partido system. The partido chief didn't care whether two or three died. When the time came to receive his cows he had to receive the same number.

I don't know about sheep; I don't about sheep. Perhaps it works the same way. I don't know. But with cattle, I know how that works.

Nasario P. García and older sisters, c. 1920–21.
Courtesy of Teodorita García-Ruelas.

19 DE MARZO DE 1992
El hijadero

Pus el hijadero era cuando estaba, cuando estaban naciendo los, . . . ésos del hijadero es los que tenían borregas. Cuando comenzaban a nacer los borreguitos, ése es el hijadero.

El dijunto Ricardo [Heller tenía] no sé qué tantas borregas. En mayo ocupaba gente, trabajadores. Y apartaban, apartaban los que iban naciendo y otros cuidaban los que iban a, a tener cuidao con los que estaban naciendo. Tenían güena sistema.

Más antes, más antes, había infinidades, munchas borregas, y sin un borrego, si un borrego se quedaba

MARCH 19, 1992
The Lambing Season

Well, the lambing season was when, when the [lambs] were being born; those who took part in the lambing season are the ones who had sheep. When the lambs started to be born, that's what's called the lambing season.

The late Ricardo [Heller], I don't know how many sheep he had. In May he hired people, workers. And what they did was to separate those lambs as they were born and others . . . took care of those that were being born. They had a good system.

Long ago, long ago there were lots of, many sheep, and if a lamb, if a lamb was left without a mother and

penco y no podían atender, se lo *daban* a la gente que lo criara. Había gente que tenía cabras. Estaban los borreguitos porque no podían atendelos, que se moría la borrega o los dejaba la borrega. Que había pencos. Se los daban a la gente. Y luego gente iba a buscar borregos pencos. Tenían cabras y se los prendían a las cabras y los criaban.

Oh, la tresquila ocupaban muchos. Güeno, yo creo que la tresquila venía cuando ya se acababa el hijadero, que ya nacían, que tenían los borreguitos las, las, eh, estas . . . yo creo que como en mayo. En abril comenzaba, y parte de mayo, el hijadero. Nomás pasaba el hijadero, la tresquila.

Sí, la lana la traiban aquí [a Albuquerque], a vender aquí al *Wool Warehouse*, o a cualesquier otra. Había dos, pero la que estuvo por años era la *Wool Warehouse*. Pero ya ora no, yo no sé qué harán con la lana. Ya se acabaron las borregas [en el Río Puerco]. Ya no admite borregas el, el gobierno en el pasteo de él. Ni cabras. Nomás vacas.

EL HIJADERO

the owners couldn't take care of it, they gave it to the people so they'd take care of it. There were people who had goats. The lambs were left alone, because the owners couldn't take care of them, because the mother would die or she abandoned them. There were orphans. Yes, they were given to the people. And then the people went looking for orphan lambs. They had goats so they'd nurse them and raise them.

Oh, for shearing, they hired a lot of men. Okay, I believe shearing time came when the lambing season was over, after the sheep gave birth to the little lambs, ah these . . . I believe it was about May. It started in April, and part of May, the lambing season. As soon as the lambing season was over, shearing started.

Yes, the wool, they brought it to be sold here [in Albuquerque], at Wool Warehouse, or some other place. There were two places, but the one that existed for years was Wool Warehouse. But as for now, I don't know what they do with the wool. There's no longer any sheep in the Río Puerco. The government doesn't permit sheep on its pastures. Nor goats. Only cows.

30 DE MARZO DE 1982
En papá estaba muy bien

Pues yo te diré, a lo que sé yo, cuando ya yo tuve edá,
que ya yo tenía diez, doce años, en de que papá
comenzó muy pobre, ya en papá corría muy güen atajo
de vacas, caballada y todo. Ya cuando yo tenía diez,
doce años en papá tenía munchas vacas. Munchas
vacas tenía. Y caballada y todo.

En papá era uno de los mejores que estaba ai en
Gualupe. Él y el dijunto Crescensio [Salas]. Pero en
papá, en papá estaba muy bien. Iba a un tiempo, iba a
un tiempo que en papá estaba muy bien.

Iba la gente, estaba muy pobre, había gente muy
pobre . . . papá cosechaba muncho trigo, maiz y de
todo. Tenía máquinas de trillar, de empacar, y
cosechaba muncho. Venía a moler pa llevar la harina
de aquí de Jémez, y la gente iba a pedile sacos de
harina, mira. Llevaban de a case, de a case en papá.
Porque había gente que estaba muy pobre. En papá les
ayudaba tamién.

Tenía munchos piones; sembraba muncho. Muy bien
estaba en papá. En un tiempo estuvo muy bien en papá.
Muy bien.

My Dad Was Very Well-Off

Well, I'll tell you. Based on what I know, when I was old enough, by the time I was ten, twelve years old, from the time Dad started very poor, to later on, Dad already had a good-size herd of cattle, horses, and all. By the time I was ten, twelve years old, Dad had a lot of cows. He had a lot of cows. Horses and all.

Dad was one of those who was much better off there in Guadalupe. He and the late Crescencio [Salas]. But Dad, Dad was very well-off. There was a time, there was a time when Dad was very well-off.

People would go, they were very poor, there were very poor people . . . Dad used to harvest a lot of wheat, corn, and everything. He had threshing and bailing machines, and he harvested a lot. He would come here to Jémez [Pueblo] to grind [the corn and wheat] to take back flour, and people would go ask him for sacks of flour. You see? They used to take from home, from Dad's place. Because there were people who were very poor, Dad would help them also.

He had lots of farmhands; he planted a lot. Dad was very well-off. At one time Dad was very well-off. Very well-off.

18 DE OCTUBRE DE 1979
Los piones

Güeno, munchas veces, munchas veces se levantaba
uno y se iba uno a escardar y loo venía uno almorzar.
Y loo se iría uno, hasta que *ya* la calor estaba muy
juerte, y loo se venía. Pero en esos tiempos, cuando yo
estaba mediano, que andaban los piones—a mí no me
tocó, es de hablar cuando yo estaba chiquito, yo me
acuerdo. Las mujeres iban, hacían pasteles, sopaipillas
y todo, y iban a llevales café allá onde estaban, a los
piones. Eso era en la tarde; en la mañana no. En la
mañana no les daban, pero en la tarde sí. A ciertas oras
iban y les llevaban café. Y esto era día por día.

Y tamién lo mesmo que cuando cortábanos zacate
nosotros allá [en Guadalupe]. Iba mamá y las
muchachas, y hasta yo, y aquí íbanos con too el
lonche [merienda], en una de esas tuallas. Aí engolvía
uno las ollas y todo pa garrale y de ai las llevaban. Los
piones no paraban hasta que llegaba uno con la comida.
Allá iba mamá a pie, a llevales a los piones.

En ese tiempo era diferente porque munchos,
munchos no cosechaban pastura y iban, y iban a
trabajar por pastura. Cuando empacaban, pus en papá
les pagaba pastura por el tiempo que le ayudaban.
[Dinero]. Muy contada la vez. Casi dinero no había en
ese tiempo muncho . . .

Farmhands

Well, many times, many times you got up and you went to hoe and then you came back to eat breakfast. And then you would go back, until the heat was *already* very hot, then you returned. But back then, when I was small, when there were farmhands—I was never a farmhand, that's to say when I was very small, I remember. The women would go, they made pies, sopaipillas, and everything, and they would take coffee to the farmhands where they were. That was in the afternoon; not in the morning. In the morning they didn't give them anything, but in the afternoon, yes. At a certain hour they'd go and take coffee to them. And this was day after day.

And the same thing was true when we used to cut grass over there in Guadalupe. My mom and the girls would go, even me, and here we went with all the lunch [snack], wrapped up in one of those dish towels. That's how you wrapped up the pans and everything to grab hold of them and that's how you carried them. The farmhands didn't stop working until you got there with the food. There went Mom on foot, to take food to the farmhands.

Back then it was different because many, many ranchers didn't harvest hay or alfalfa and they went, and they went and worked in exchange for hay or alfalfa. Whenever they did any bailing, well my dad paid the farmhands hay in exchange for the length of time they helped. [Money]. Very rarely. There was hardly much money back then . . .

Threshing Beans. Teodorita García, Antonio García (on horseback),
Ramón García, and Nasario P. García on fence post, c. 1920–21.
Courtesy of Teodorita García-Ruelas.

18 DE OCTUBRE DE 1979
¡Allá se daban unas siembras que déjate!

[Sembraban] frijol, maiz y calabazas. Eso jue cuando ya no hubo agua en la cequia, pero cuando, cuando en el tiempo que yo estaba muy mediano, esto era cuando yo estaba muy chiquito, que había agua en la cequia. Antonces tenían el atarque. Sembraban alfarfa, sembraban trigo, maiz, de todo. Pero en ese tiempo, cuando yo estaba muy mediano, la gente, pus no había máquinas pa cortar, ni nada. Con el hoz. Se juntaban cinco y seis piones, con la mano cortaban el trigo y loo lo trillaban con caballos.

OCTOBER 18, 1979
The Crops Raised over There Were Really Something!

People planted pinto beans, corn, and pumpkins. That happened when water no longer ran in the ditch; but when, when I was very small, when I was very small, that's when water did run in the ditch. That's when people had the reservoir. People planted alfalfa, they planted wheat, corn, and everything. But during that time, when I was very small, well, people didn't have machinery [for cutting or bailing alfalfa], or anything. With the sickle. Five or six farmhands would get together, and they cut the wheat by hand and then they'd thresh it with horses.

Güeno. El frijol cuando ya estaba maduro, tenía uno que levantarse, a que no se desgranara, muy de mañana, con el rocío, arrancalo y lo hacía uno montones. Y ai lo dejaba uno. Cuando ya estaba listo, que quedaba, que acababa uno, pues ya iba uno. Echaba uno una lona, en el carro, con dos o tres umentos, y lo iba echando uno en el carro.

Y de ai le daba uno pal era. Y ai lo trillaba uno con caballos. En ese tiempo tenía en papá una máquina pa trillar el frijol. Después de que lo machucaban con los caballos, le quitaban lo grueso con la orquilla, y iba quedando el frijol. Y loo cuando ya acababan, pus, lo metían a la trilladora, una chiquita, a juerza de mano le daba uno.

La trilladora esa tenía como uno o dos o tres cedazos: el primero apartaba lo grueso; el segundo apartaba ya lo más delgadito; y luego el otro apartaba lo más fino y nomás el frijol caiba pa bajo. Tenía tres cedazos. Ya los caballos no era más que machucaran lo más grueso.

Ése es el trigo, y el frijol tamién, pero casi pa quitale lo grueso, eh, con una pala de tabla. Ésa la quitaba [la paja] y ai volaba muncho, ¿ves? Todo lo que podía y loo lo metían a la trilladora. Lo mismo el trigo.

¡Oh! ¡Allá se daban unas siembras que déjate! Las milpas crecían del tamaño de esta casa. Y de *temporal*, no, no de regadío. Calabazas, ¡asina grandes [15–20 libras]!

Okay. The bean crop, when it was ripe, one had to get up very early, when the dew was still fresh, so the bean plants wouldn't fall apart, to pull them out and then make small piles with them. You left the bean crop there. When it was ready to load, when you were done picking and piling it, you went on to the next step. You'd spread a canvas on a horse wagon, with two or three sideboards, and then you proceeded to load up the bean crop.

From there you headed for the threshing machine. After the horses crushed the bean plants, the thick part of the plant was removed with a pitchfork, and the bean itself was separated. And when people were finished, well, they'd put the pinto beans in the small thresher, all by hand.

That thresher had about two or three sieves: the first one separated the thick part of the plant; the second one separated the thinner portions; and then the third one separated the finer parts, and only the beans dropped to the bottom of the thresher, where they were collected. The thresher had three sieves. All the horses did was to walk on the bean plants.

As for the wheat, you do the same thing also, but almost always for separating the thick part of the bean plant, ah, you used a wooden shovel. That's what you used to separate the "straw" as it flew away, you see? Whatever you could separate, you did so, and the rest you put it then in the thresher. You did the same thing with the bean plants as with wheat.

The crops raised over there were really something! The corn fields grew as tall as this house. And from rainfall, not, not from irrigation. Pumpkins this big [15–20 pounds]!

Nasario García and cousin Julia García in front of the Nasario P.
García and Teodoro García horno, Guadalupe, c. 1938.

18 DE OCTUBRE DE 1979
Hacían pan en el horno

Lo que era como en octubre, noviembre, la gente empacaba muncho. Y luego cuando ya, el tiempo estaba, pus mataban una vaca. Hacían cecinas. Mataban cochinos. Ya ellos estaban aprevenidos de comida por todo el invierno.

Antonces eh, antonces eh, no había conque el botito de dos libras. ¡De cincuenta de manteca! Sí. Por todo el invierno. Carne seca, sacos asina [grandotes]. ¡Mira! Dos, tres sacos de carne seca. Todo el invierno. No había yeleras . . . en el invierno no se hacía nada,

OCTOBER 18, 1979
They Baked Bread in the Bee-Hive Oven

Like now in October, November, people would can a lot. And then, when the right time came, well, they slaughtered a cow. They made pieces of jerky. They butchered hogs. And then people were set with food for the entire winter.

Back then, ah, back then ah, there was no messing around with two-pound cans. Fifty pounds of lard! Yes. For the whole winter. Dried beef, huge sacks. Look. Two, three sacks of jerky. For the whole winter. There were no refrigerators . . . in winter it [food] didn't spoil, because people had a little room ["dispensary," usually

porque la gente tenía un cuartito [dispensa] con ese fin. En el invierno cuando ya comenzaba el frío, ese cuartito, ése siempre estaba, primeramente cuando ya venía el frío, pus la carne estaba helada.

Pero comida, ¡déjate! De comida en ese tiempo [la Depresión], cuando los tiempos duros, los que vivían en la Plaza [en Albuquerque], eran los que estaban sufriendo. Los que estábanos en los ranchos, no. Porque allá había, aí tenían tantas vacas de leche. Y luego cosechaban harina de maiz; la llevaban y la molían y hacían atole y de maneras que de comida la gente no, no sufría de comida.

Aá en esos tiempos había más comida que lo que tiene uno aquí ora que está cerquita de la tienda. Porque aquí va uno por la torta de pan y cuando ya se la acaba, va por lotra, ¿ves? Nos está la tienda. Aá no. Aá no. Echaban pan las mujeres. Aá no, no se compraba nada.

Pues, eh, yo estaba muy chiquito. En papá cosechaba trigo en ese tiempo, pero en papá en ese tiempo estaba bien. Y era el único que tenía una máquina pa cortar el trigo, de caballos. Y luego, de ai como te digo yo, lo trillaban en la era, de caballos. Y luego de ai cuando ya lo echaban en sacos y todo, veníanos a un molino, que lo manejaban con la agua, aquí a Jémez. Sí. Ai veníanos. Estaba chiquito yo.

Y pan. Hacían pan en el horno. Del modo que hacían, que le echaban lumbre al horno, que se calentara bien. Y loo cuando ya estaba listo pa echar, porque estaba poco grande, como ora la mesa, aí echaban el pan, es decir, el pan. O luego aquí le ponían unos adobes y traiban un, hacían zoquete, y le tapaban bien. Y lo dejaban hasta ciertas horas. Con el puro calor, el calor del horno, no brasas. Lo barrían. Lo

separate from the house] with that aim in mind. In the winter when the cold came, that little room, that was already prepared, especially by the time it got cold, why the meat was frozen.

But food, wow! When it came to food during that time [the Great Depression], when times were rough, those who lived in Albuquerque were the ones suffering. Those of us who were on the ranches, not so. Because over there we had, there they had so many milk cows. And then they raised corn flour; they took the corn, had it ground, and made corn gruel from it, so when it came to food the people didn't, didn't suffer from lack of it.

Back in those days there was more food than what you have here now that you're closer to a store. Because here when you go for a loaf of bread and when it's gone, you go after another one, understand? The store's right there for us. Not over there. The women baked bread. Over there, you didn't buy anything.

Well, ah, I was very small. Dad used to harvest wheat back then, but Dad back in those days was well-off. And he was the only one who had a wheat-cutting machine, pulled by horses. And then, as I'm telling you, they'd thresh the wheat with horses in the threshing area. And then from there they would put it in sacks and everything. They came to the grinding mill, run by water here in Jémez Pueblo. Yes. That's where we came. I was very small.

And bread. They [women] made bread in the bee-hive oven. The way they used to do it is that they'd build a fire in the oven, till it was hot. Then when the dough was all ready to put in, because the oven was pretty big, like this table, that's where they put in the bread, that is, the dough. Then they would cover the entrance

barrían. Pero estaba caliente. Pero lo barrían pronto, bien barrido, y luego lo echaban [la masa], y loo lo tapaban bien [el horno] que no saliera calor aquí en la puertecita. Cuando ya estaba [el pan], que se consideraba que ya estaba, quitaban el ése [los adobes] y pus salía el pan. No se quemaba. Con el puro calor del adobe. Con la pala esa [de madera] sacaban las charolas [de pan].

HACÍAN PAN EN EL HORNO

to the oven with adobes and they would bring, they would mix mud, and cover the oven's entrance well. And they left it like that for so many hours, cooking the bread. With just the heat, just the heat of the oven, not even ashes. They'd clean it out. They'd clean it out. But it was hot. But they would sweep it right away, really good, and then they put in [the dough]; then they would cover the oven, the little door's entrance, very well, so the heat wouldn't escape. When the bread was ready, when they thought it was about ready, they would remove the adobes from the entrance and the bread was taken out. It wouldn't burn. It baked just from the heat. They would take the bread out with wooden shovels.

La matanza. The Teodoro García family, Guadalupe, c. 1922–24.
Courtesy of Teodorita García-Ruelas.

19 DE MARZO DE 1992
La matanza

Pa matar un marrano, eso venía como en eh, en diciembre, dígase, o a últimos de octubre, cuando ya comenzaba el frío. Ponían barriles y los llenaban de agua y les echaban cal y cuando lo mataban [el marrano] lo tendían en unas tablas. Le echaban agua y lo tapaban con guangoches o lonas y lo dejaban, y loo lo pelaban. Eso era too lo que hacían.

Después de que lo mataban, lo volteaban boca abajo en unas tablas y le quitaban la lonja. Lo que es la manteca. Y loo de ai, lo eh, hacían las tiras de

MARCH 19, 1992
Butchering

When the time came to butcher a hog, that was about, ah, in December, let us say, or toward the end of October, when the cold weather set in. Barrels full of water were set up and lye put in them, and when the hog was butchered, it was laid out on boards. They poured water on it, and they covered it with gunny sacks or canvases, and they let it sit, and then they scraped off the bristle.

After it was butchered, the hog was turned face down on some boards and the fat was removed, which is where the lard comes from. And from there they'd cut the strips of fat, along with the skin. Then they would

manteca, contoy cuero. Y loo le quitaban la manteca y le dejaban nomás el puro cuero; se quedaba el puro cuero. Los cueros los guardaban pa frijoles, pa cocer frijoles. Y la manteca, hacían chicharrones con ella.

Estaban unos deslonjando . . . la manteca y la echaban en un cajete o lo que juera y aquéllos estaban haciendo chicharrones. Cortándola [la lonja]. Nomás la cortaban y la echaban en la olla pa, pa los chicharrones. Quedaba nomás el puro cuero.

Las mujeres lo que hacían es que agarraban toda la sangre y ellas la benificiaban, apartaban ciertas tripas, pa hacer morcillas. Ellas tenían que saber cuáles [tripas] eran güenas.

[La cabeza] y hasta las patas [se salvaba]. ¡Todo! La única cosa que se tiraba era la panza. Eso sí, del marrano. La de res, esa sí la pelaban; esa sí. Pero no de marrano. De marrano nomás agarraban las tripas que necitaban. Ya ellas [las mujeres] sabían pa hacer morcillas. Me acuerdo que de esas tripas tenían que descogelas.

Pus casi, cuasi aá en los ranchos mataban los animales cuando ya venía el tiempo frío, que ya estaba llegando el invierno, porque no había yeleras. Cuando ya estaba frío.

Es más simple matar una vaca. No es tanto trabajo. En tres horas se acababa todo, porque de una vaca no hay ni chicharrones. Carne seca y too eso [sí].

take off the fat and the only thing left was the skin; only the skin was left. The strips of skin were saved for pinto beans, whenever they were cooked, and from the fat part they'd make *chicharrones* [cracklings].

Some men would be taking off the strips of fat, ah, and then they tossed them into a tin tub or whatever, while others were making chicharrones. They did this by cutting the strips of fat. All they did was to cut them off and they'd toss them into the pan for chicharrones. Only the skin was left.

What the women did was to catch the blood, and they made use of it. They'd set aside certain intestines, so as to make blood sausage. The women had to know which intestines were the good ones.

The head was used and even the feet. Everything! The only thing that was tossed away was the stomach. That we did. The hog's stomach. As for the cow's head, that we used. We scraped and cleaned it; we utilized it. But not the hog's stomach. As for the hog, people only saved the intestines they needed; the women already knew which ones to set aside for blood sausage. I remember that they had to choose from the intestines.

Well, out on the ranches people almost, almost always slaughtered animals when the cold weather hit, when winter was beginning to set in, because there weren't any refrigerators. When the cold came!

It's a lot more simple to slaughter a cow. It's not as much work. In three hours everything was over with, because from a cow you don't have chicharrones. Only dried meat [jerky] and that sort of thing.

Juan Córdova home, built 1900, Placita of Guadalupe.

19 DE MARZO DE 1992
Tiendas y trigo

Pus, ya, cuando en papá trabajaba aá en Salazar, que comenzó, ¡oh!, ésos eran munchos, munchos años atrás. Hasta el tiempo que nací yo . . . Cuando ya yo, que me acuerdo, el único que tenía tienda era don Crescensio Salas. Y este, ¿cómo se llama? Ai en Gualupe. ¿Quién era? No me acuerdo cómo se llamaba, ¡hombre! ¡Don Juan Córdova! Don Juan Córdova.

[Don Élfego Aranda]. Sí. Ora al último. Sí. No me acuerdo. No me acuerdo, pero eso jue, oh, no me acuerdo. ¿Del '38, el '40? Tenía tienda el dijunto

MARCH 19, 1992
Stores and Wheat

Well, when Dad already worked there in Salazar, when he got started, oh!, that was many, many years ago. Even before I was born . . . When I already, . . . as to what I remember, the only one who had a store was Don Crescensio Salas. And, what's his name? There in Guadalupe. Who was it? Man, I can't remember what his name was. Don Juan Córdova! Don Juan Córdova.

Don Élfego Aranda also. But that was much later, yes. I don't recall when. I don't remember when, but that was, oh, I don't recall. From thirty-eight, from forty onward? That's when the late Élfego Aranda had a

Élfego. Pero ése jue de los últimos. Ya ni don Juan Córdova ni don Crescencio tenían tiendas.

La tienda que tenía el dijunto Ricardo [Heller en Cabezón] era nomás provisión como harina, manteca, café y cosas asina.

Cuando había agua en la cequia que cosechaban trigo, iban a Jémez a moler [trigo]. Yo tendría como, como doce años. Me acuerdo. Yo llegué ir con en papá. No sé qué año. No sé qué año sería. Pero iba muncha gente que cosechaba trigo. Iban a moler a Jémez. No sé cómo se arreglarían. Pienso que les daban harina o cambio. Había un molino ai.

[La gente de Guadalupe] iba por ai por la Cañada del Camino, y loo bajaba uno al, al, eh, por Cucho, que le decían. Y venía uno a salir a San Ysidro, por el Río Salao. Yo me acuerdo que en un viaje se tardarían como, como un día y poquito más. En la noche cuando se hacía oscuro, aí tenían que dormir. Si venían a moler sí iban derecho a Jémez.

Venían [también a Albuquerque] toda la Cañada del Camino y venían por el Empedrao, Bernalillito, y por la Ceja y venían a salir aquí a Corrales. Un día y medio [se tardaban]. Menos a Jémez.

[En Albuquerque] había tiendas. Estaba el eh, el Franchini. Estaba el Vayo. Tiendas muy grandes ai. Ai comprábanos. El Massaglias. Sí. El Massaglias. ¡Oh! Pero . . . ora al último, en el cuarenta y cuatro [paraba la gente en la tienda de Eddy García en Candelaria].

store. But he was one of the last ones. By that time neither Don Juan Córdova nor Don Crescensio Salas had stores.

The store that the late Ricardo Heller had in Cabezón was only for staples like flour, lard, coffee, and things like that.

When water ran in the ditch, when people raised wheat, they went to Jémez Pueblo to grind it. I must have been about, about twelve years old. I remember that I got to go with Dad. I don't know what year. I don't know what year that was. But a lot of people who raised wheat used to go. They went to grind it in Jémez Pueblo. I don't know what kind of arrangement they had with the Indians. I believe they paid them in cash or with flour.

People from Guadalupe went by way of La Cañada del Camino. And then you went down through, through, Cucho, as it was called. And you ended up coming out in San Ysidro, across the Río Salado. I remember that trip must have taken about, about a little bit more than a day. Oh yes! At night when it got dark on you, that's where you slept. But if the people came to grind wheat in Jémez Pueblo, they headed straight for the pueblo.

Whenever people came to Albuquerque, they did so by way of La Cañada del Camino, El Empedrao, Bernalillito, and by way of La Ceja, ending up here in Corrales. They'd take a day and a half. Less to Jémez Pueblo.

In Albuquerque there were stores. There was, ah, Franchini's. There was Vayo's. Very large stores. That's where we shopped. At Massaglias's. Yes. At Massaglias's. Oh! Toward the end, in forty-four people used to stop at Eddy García's in Candelaria.

19 DE MARZO DE 1992
Ponían trampas

Pus, eh, muncha gente, lo hacía. De noviembre pa
adelante, lo que era hasta febrero, ponían trampas
porque se vendían los cueros, de los coyotes. Y loo los
desollaban al revés, y loo los ponían en una estaca, que
se secaran. Y pagaban muy bien.

Estaba la zalellería [Wool Warehouse]. Y había otra;
había dos. Güeno, [pagaban] asegún. No me acuerdo
exaito qué; no te poo decir qué tanto. No me acuerdo,
porque yo nunca cacé eso que yo vide, pero pueda que
tres o cuatro pesos. Yo no sé. ¡O más! No sé.

Casi en papá en eso no, no tenía muncho tiempo de
andar pasando, pero había munchos otros: los
Jaramillo, los Valencia y todos. Los que no tenían
muncho que atender, cuando ya levantaban la cosecha,
porque como ora en papá y munchos que sembraban
muncho, estaban muy ocupaos too el invierno
deshojando y desgranando maiz y trillando frijol y too
eso. No tenían tiempo de eh, de eh, de poner trampas.
Pero otros sí. ¡Oh! Ésos sí ponían hasta cien trampas.

[Cazaban] los coyotes y ah, ¿cómo le nombran
aquéllos? Güeno, munchas veces tocaba que agarraban
de esas zorras. Tejones no los dejaban cazar. Y no sé
qué otro animal. No me acuerdo. Lo más que había era
zorras, de vez en cuando. Coyotes, eso era lo más que
había.

MARCH 19, 1992
They'd Set Traps

Well, ah, many people, did it. From November onward,
up to February, ranchers set traps because they sold the
coyotes' hides. They'd skin the coyotes and turn the
hides inside out, and then they'd put the hides on a
stake so they'd dry. And they used to pay very well for
them.

There was the tannery, Wool Warehouse [in
Albuquerque]. And there was another one; there were
two of them. Okay, they paid accordingly for hides. I
don't remember exactly how much; I can't tell you
how much. I don't remember, because I never hunted
those animals I saw, but perhaps they paid three or four
dollars. I don't know. Or more. I don't know.

My dad hardly did that. He didn't have much time to
spare, but there were others who did have time: the
Jaramillos, the Valencias and everyone else. Those who
didn't have much to tend to, once they had picked
their crops, because, now my dad and others who
planted, they were very busy in the winter chucking
and grinding corn and threshing pinto beans and all
that sort of thing. They didn't have time to ah, to ah,
to set traps. But others did. Oh! Those who did have
time set as many as one hundred traps.

They caught the coyotes and, ah, what did they call
those others? Okay, often times they'd catch those
female foxes. You couldn't hunt badgers. And I don't
know what other animal. I don't recall. What you
found most, once in a while, were female foxes.
Coyotes, that's what you found most of!

19 DE MARZO DE 1992
Limpiando la cequia

A mí se me hace que si no estoy equívoco, en marzo. Güeno, pus, eh, el mayordomo era el que iba limpiar la cequia. El mayordomo era como patrón. Tenía una vara que le midían la distancia [a la gente]. "Aquí limpias tú." Y le midía al otro y le midía al otro y le midía al otro.

Y loo según estaba tenían que sacar. Algunos le decían [a la persona]: "Tienes que dale dos clavadas." Lo que es la pala, y barrida . . . Clava tú lo que es toda la pala. Eso es una clavada. Y luego la barrida es sacar la tierra floja. El ensolve, tierra, tierra. Se ensolvaba y tenían que sacale tierra a la cequia.

Oh sí, pus iba uno adelante limpiando la cizaña y los otros que venían iban limpiando la cequia.

Cleaning the Ditch

I believe, if I'm not mistaken, it was in March. Okay, well, ah, as a result of the mayordomo they [the farmers] went and helped clean the ditch. The mayordomo was like a boss. He had a yardstick that he measured the distance with. "Here's what you'll clean." And he'd measure for this one, that one, and the other.

And then, depending on the ditch's condition, you had to dig. Some would say: "You have to give it two spades, that is, the depth of the shovel, and a sweeping . . . , you had to dig the entire depth of the shovel. That's a spade. And then the sweeping is to dig out the loose dirt, the residue, dirt and more dirt. It would back up and form a residue, and they had to dig out the dirt.

Why, there was someone ahead cleaning the tumbleweeds, and those who followed cleaned out the ditch.

II
A World of Ambivalence, 1923–1928

Adolescence in rural Hispanic communities like Guadalupe was compressed into the years from eleven to fifteen. During my father's adolescence, the midtwenties, the population of Guadalupe remained quite stable. Only two families appear to have abandoned the village; one was my parents' future godparents (*padrinos*) by marriage, Jesús and Perfilia Córdova, who moved to Bernalillo after he was maimed in the war; the other family settled in Albuquerque in 1928, where the husband found a job at the Santa Fe Railroad, commonly known among Hispanics as "Los Shopes," or "the Shops."

Those who remained in Guadalupe continued to live off the land and their livestock. Even though prices then, compared to today's, were modest at best, some *guadalupanos*, such as my grandparents, were able to sell a few cattle as well as crops. A cow back then sold for about ten dollars, a bale of hay for twenty to twenty-five cents, and a fifty-gallon barrel of ground corn went for one dollar. Severe droughts, which played havoc with both rancher and farmer alike, came later, in the midthirties.

Since then times have changed, to say the least. The story "Más antes había crianza" ("Long Ago There Was Respect") laments a disappearing custom in modern times, because in Guadalupe respect permeated the entire community. No one commanded more of it than the older men and women (*hombres grandes y mujeres de edad*) or the local priest. Veneration for the priest is evident in "Diezmos y primicias" ("Tithes and First Fruits"). Mutual respect between priests and parishioners has also waned since those days, however, and only cash donations are used to support local church traditions and activities. Crops in lieu of money are a thing of the past, even in the rural areas of New Mexico.

Some celebrations combined the secular and the relig-

ious and were celebrated whether the priest's monthly visit to Guadalupe coincided with them or not. The most popular of the festive days was Saint John's Day, June 24 ("El Día de San Juan"); there would be a mass (if the priest came), rooster racing (a misnomer) or *corridas del gallo*, horse races, and other activities, all of which culminated in a dance that began in the evening at the local *sala*, or dance hall (see figure 1) and lasted sometimes until sunrise the next day. Similar events, except for the rooster racing, were held on Saint Anne's Day, July 26. This day was reserved for women; men stayed in the background.

Several kinds of events brought the community together, to be sure, but none conjured up more excitement than weddings ("Los casorios"). Everyone became intimately involved, from the oldest *abuelita* to the youngest grandchild, from sunrise until early dawn the next day. The same thing was essentially true of the Stations of the Cross during Holy Week, as well as of the celebration of Nuestra Señora de Guadalupe ("La Virgen"), the community's patron saint, although the atmosphere in both of these cases was more solemn.

It is important to note that the religious functions (*funciones*) rendered the communities and their organizers, many of them prominent members, highly visible. Whatever tone and example they set for the community tended to filter on down to the children, including adolescents. As children grew older, whether male or female, they became more involved in church matters, whether as an altar boy or as a member of the choir. This kind of involvement taught young people social and religious responsibility, self-discipline, and respect, all of which served on occasion as substitutes for formal education.

But church affairs also encouraged commingling. First

Holy Communion served as a kind of "graduation," since very few adolescents ever graduated from the eighth grade, the highest level of education then accessible. Moreover religious functions, in addition to local dances, offered young people an opportunity to strike up special friendships.

A more subdued but joyous time of the year, as we learn from my father, and more of a family affair, was Christmastime ("Los Crismes"). This privacy aspect also extended somewhat to a death in a family, but grief and bereavement gripped members of the whole village and sometimes reached beyond, as seen in "Un entierro" ("A Burial").

While death evoked sadness, the birth of a child engendered joy and happiness. The purveyor of this good news was customarily the midwife ("Una partera"). She served as the pediatrician many years ago, whereas the task of caring for the ill fell on the shoulders of the *curanderas*, or folk healers. At least one folk healer could be found in every community. She resembled a general practitioner, whose responsibilities encompassed treating ailments that ran the gamut from colds ("Resfríos"), indigestion ("El empacho"), to fright ("Una solevada") or the evil eye ("El mal ojo").

But the kaleidoscope of activities observed by an adolescent on the farm formed only part of his young life. Young people also heard stories about ghosts, witches, or imaginary animals. Encounters with some of these creatures, as in "Un bulto negro" ("A Black Shape") were an integral and vivid part of growing up; my father related this story to me numerous times when I was a small child. Others, for example "Dos brujas y dos juanes" ("Two Witches and Two Juans"), were stories his father had told him.

Adolescence on the farm or ranch was an ambivalent period in the lives of young people in the Río Puerco valley, but exciting because by virtue of more, yet still limited, parental freedom and personal inquisitiveness, it expanded the opportunities to explore a cultural world in part unknown to them, or at least not completely understood. In rural Hispanic communities like Guadalupe, adolescence was a universe unto its own, filled with traditions that simultaneously fused and separated the real and the imagined.

Nasario "Junie" García, Guadalupe, c. 1945.

19 DE MARZO DE 1992
Más antes había crianza

No. Ya eso no. Más antes había respeto. Si un mayor le mandaba a uno que hiciera alguna cosa, no había quién le rezongara, que le dijiera nada, porque había respeto. Eh, a la comparación de ora. Si, si uno le va decir [algo] algún muchacho se voltea y le dice "tú pallá, tú pacá." Y más antes no. Más antes había crianza, respeto. Muy diferente.

En un modo, en un modo, era que, que ese modo, ese costumbre tenía la gente de más de enseñar a, a su familia de ese modo. Es el modo que todas las cosas. Es

MARCH 19, 1992
Long Ago There Was Respect

No. That's no longer true. Long ago there was respect. If an adult asked you to do something, to do something, there was no answering back, no nothing, because there was respect. Ah, in comparison to now. If, if one is going to tell some young man something, he'll turn around and tell you this or that. And long ago that was not the case. Long ago there was respect. It was very different.

In a way, in a way, it was that, it was that the habit, the custom was people's way of doing things, of teaching their children certain ways. That's the way things were. It's the same thing as if I raised a dog and

lo mesmo que si yo crío un perro y le abro la puerta y lo dejo que ande en la calle; nunca lo voy a sujetar en la yarda porque quiere salirse. Pero la gente, eh, antes, le daban crianza a la familia, y que hubiera respeto, y le respondiera bien a la gente mayor.

Ya no hay nada de eso. Ya no hay nada de eso. Antes, otra cosa, muy diferente antes a ora. Más antes si uno hacía mal, el padre agarraba una faja y le pegaba con una cuarta o lo que juera, a la familia. Ora no pueden porque la ley se metió de que no tienen derecho de ejecutalos. Y ai es onde agarraron más alas la juventú. La ley tiene la culpa hoy en día, de que ai andan sueltos y no les dicen anda. Y si van y los pescan y les pegan [los padres], los encierran. ¿Cómo le llaman eso? *Child abuse.* ¿Quién tiene la culpa? La ley. Y más antes no. El padre tenía la ley, pa ejecutar a sus hijos. La ley no se metía en eso. Por eso había crianza.

No había quién se portara mal al padre y la madre porque, eh, le tenían respeto al padre y a la madre. Ora no hay respeto ni hay miedo tampoco. Ya ora lo que hacen todos los días sale en las nuevas, uno atrás de otro. Si un muchacho lo va a recomunir el padre o la madre por alguna cosa, se encapricha. Nomás esperan a que se duerman y loo vienen y los matan. Más antes, nunca se vido eso.

I opened the gate and let him roam out in the street. I'm never going to hold him back in the yard because he wants to go out. But people, ah, long ago, showed their family discipline, so that there was respect, so they answered adults properly.

That's no longer the case. That's long gone. Long ago, it was different, very different from now. Long ago if you did something wrong, the father got out the belt and he'd whip the culprit in the family with a quirt or whatever. Now you can't because the law has intervened, saying parents don't have the right to discipline their children. And that's where the young people of today have gotten wise. The law is at fault nowadays, and that's the reason young people run around loose and nobody says anything to them. And if parents go and catch them and whip them, they get locked up. What do they call that? Child abuse. Who's at fault? The law. And long ago that wasn't the case. The father ruled; he disciplined his children. The law didn't meddle. That's the reason there was respect.

There wasn't anybody who misbehaved with the father or the mother because, ah, ah, they respected the father and mother. Now there's no respect, nor fear either. Now whatever happens every day, it comes out in the news, one thing after another. If the father or mother is going to scold a son for something, he resents it. Then all he does is wait till they're asleep, and he kills them. Long ago you didn't see that sort of thing.

18 DE OCTUBRE DE 1979
Diezmos y primicias

Una vez al mes y el padre venía de Cuba. En un boguecito de un caballo. Antonces en ese tiempo no usaban el dinero. El padre coletaba maiz, ristras de chile, frijol, o lo que le dieran . . . Como ora lo que nosotros echamos en las carteritas, que antonces le decían diezmos y primicias. Como es pa las fiestas. Un barril de maiz. Los mayordomos juntaban. Aquí andamos juntando la primicia. El que tenía un peso, daba un peso. El que tenía un bote de veinte, de cincuenta de frijol, o cincuenta libras. Eso le daban. O un barril de maiz. Y ai iba [uno] echando, ves, pa cuando venía el padre. Todo eso era del padre. ¡Pa que mires tú! Años, años pasaos. Pos, de todo recogían; dinero y lo que juera. Ora no. Ora va una a misa, ¡qué esperanza! Tiene que ser *cash*. [Los diezmos y primicias eran] pa las fiestas. Pa las fiestas.

Sí, pus, daban sus coletas [una vez al mes]. Dos reales. Antonces casi sí echaban sus dos reales o lo que . . . casi la gente ya sabía. Orraba dos reales, quince centavos, lo que juera. Pus antonces dos reales, ¡qué bárbaro! Eran como cinco pesos.

Casi los padres eran ya con edá. [Eran] americanos. Yo no llegué a ver mexicanos. Sí sabían [español]. Sí. En mexicano. Todo en mexicano. Aá no se costumbraba en inglés.

OCTOBER 18, 1979
Tithes and First Fruits

Once a month the priest came from Cuba. In a one-horse buggy. Back in those days, they didn't use money. The priest collected corn, strings of chile, pinto beans, or whatever they gave him ... Like now what we give in the little envelopes, back then they were called tithes and first fruits. Like for the fiestas. A barrel of corn. The mayordomos collected it. Here we were all collecting tithes. He who had a dollar, gave a dollar. The one who had a twenty-pound or a fifty-pound can of pinto beans, that's what he gave. Or a barrel of corn. And that's the way the mayordomo did it, you see, by the time the priest came. All that belonged to the priest. Just imagine! That was years and years ago. Yes, why people gathered all kinds of stuff; money or whatever. No more. Now you go to church, and no such luck! It has to be cash. That was only during the fiestas. Only during the fiestas.

[Otherwise] people did put money in the collection basket. Two bits. Then people did put in their twenty-five cents or what ... people already knew what to do. They'd save twenty-five cents, fifteen cents, or whatever. Back then, twenty-five cents, good gracious, it was about five dollars [today]!

They [the priests], were not very young. Most of them were already older. They were Americans. I never got to see "Mexicans."

Oh yes! They knew Spanish. Yes. They gave mass in Spanish. Everything was in Spanish. English was not used over there.

18 DE OCTUBRE DE 1979
El Día de San Juan

En el verano festejaban el día de San Juan. El día de Santa Ana. Ésos eran los días que festejaban, como era en el verano.

Güeno. El día de San Juan, pus, iban a misa y luego entre el día, después del mediodía, tenían baile, corrían gallo, o corrían carreras de caballo. Pero lo más que corrían, gallo, el día de San Juan.

Enterraban el gallo, y el que lo sacaba, ése salía a juir con él y los demás lo alcanzaban a ver si se lo podían quitar. Y el que lo quitara, güeno, el que iba con el gallo, pos, el que iba a quitárselo, les daba con él. Y si aquél podía quitárselo, pos él le daba con el gallo hasta que no dejaban nada. ¿Y sabes tú cómo le quitaba el gallo? El que iba con el gallo, que iba a dale aquél, porque el otro se iba, con las riendas. Agarraban las riendas y se las agarraban asina [como un lazo]. Tenían ideas. Si no le quitaban el gallo, pus ése ganaba, ¿ves? Yo estaba muy mediano toavía.

El que sí me acuerdo toavía que le llegué a ver, que estaba más grande que yo, mi compadre Salvador [Gonzales]. Mi compadre Salvador era güeno pa prenderse a caballo pa sacar un gallo.

Pero las fiestas, las fiestas, cuando venían, eran en noviembre. Pus, en esos tiempos se juntaba la gente, pa las fiestas. Iba el padre, y, está la iglesia, y loo daban güelta con la procesión, pero en ese tiempo ponían luminarias. ¿Tú sabes lo que es luminarias? *Todo* lo que es alrededor. Cuando ya iban a salir con la procesión, iba uno adelante prendiéndoles con tiempo. De maneras que cuando el padre salía y la gente, iban

OCTOBER 18, 1979
Saint John's Day

In the summer they would celebrate Saint John's Day
[June 24]. Saint Anne's Day. Those were the days they
celebrated, that were in the summer.

Okay. On Saint John's Day, well, people went to
mass and then during the day, after midday, they had a
dance, rooster racing, or horse races. But what they did
most on Saint John's Day was, rooster racing.

They'd bury the rooster, and the one who plucked it
out of the ground, that one [the *gallero*] took off
galloping, and the rest of the pack would try to wrest it
from him. And the one who could take the rooster
away from the one who had it, okay, well, the ones
who were going to take it away from the *gallero*, he'd
hit them with it. And if someone tried to take it away
from him, he'd strike them with it, till there was
nothing left of the rooster. And do you know how they
took away the rooster? The one who had the rooster,
who was going to hit somebody with it, because
someone went after him, this *gallero* would use the
reins. They would use the reins in the form of a loop,
like a rope. They had their tricks. If nobody wrested
the rooster from him, why he'd win, see? I was still
very small.

The one I still do remember seeing, who was older
than me, was my compadre Salvador [Gonzales]. My
compadre Salvador was good at leaning down from his
galloping horse and plucking out the rooster.

But the fiestas, the *fiestas*, when they came, that
was in November [in honor of the Virgin of Guadalupe;
later changed to December 12]. Well, back then people

por entre medio de las luminarias, y se alumbraba. Sí.
En las vísperas, cuando sacaban, cuando sacaban la
procesión.

got together for the fiestas. The priest went, and, there's the church, and then people circled it with their procession, but in those days they set out luminarias. You know what luminarias are? *All* around the church. When they were about to start the procession, someone went ahead of it lighting the luminarias, so that when the priest and people started, they went alongside the luminarias, one by one, and everything lit up. Yes. During vespers, that's when, that's when the procession started.

Nasario P. García and Agapita López, 1935.

18 DE OCTUBRE DE 1979
Los casorios

Cuando había casorios, yo te voy a decir cómo hacían. Eso jue, años, años. Yo estaba chiquito. Antonces no había más del carro de caballos. En ese tiempo iban los músicos en un carro adelante y los novios y los padrinos en otro. Y loo de ai la gente a caballo y la carrería atrás. En ese tiempo, pus, fíjate tú, traiban violín y guitarra, y pos, la gente tenía gusto. Estaba con vida la gente. No ora como que estamos muertos. Con pistolas, oye, tirando balazos y todo. ¡Uh! ¡Déjate! Lo mesmo que ver un *show* de *cowboys* ai. La mesma

OCTOBER 18, 1979
Weddings

Whenever there were weddings, I'm going to tell you how they did it. That was years, years ago. I was very small. Back then all there was was the horse wagon. In those days the musicians rode a horse wagon in front, and the bride and groom and the godparents in another right behind the musicians. And then the people on horseback and the rest of the wagons followed. In those days, well, just imagine, the musicians had violin and guitar, and, well, people enjoyed themselves. People had life. Not like now; we're all dead. Listen, with pistols, firing and everything. Yeah! No kidding. The same thing as watching a cowboy show. The same

cuenta. Asina se acostumbraba más antes. Sí. En los bailes, la mesma cosa. Pero no había quién matara a naiden. La gente era diferente, pero ése era su vida de la gente.

Los ranchos estaban destendidos, retiraos, y diondequiera venían. De todos los ranchos, y ai [en Guadalupe] se juntaban. En la iglesia onde había misa. En la noche.

Vestían nomás con sus calzones de lona, sombrero, y todo. Eh, las mujeres, había otro estilo pa las mujeres. Las mujeres no usaban en ese tiempo pantalones. Ésos no se conocían antonces. Túnicos, sí. Cabello largo . . . se costumbraba muncho el vestido largo.

Oh, los bailes ya nomás a poquito de que se metiera el sol, haciéndose oscuro, y duraban. Había veces que duraban, hasta las cuatro de la madrugada, las tres de la mañana. ¡Oh sí! No tenían fin.

El que tenía sala, y tenía una tienda tamién, el dijunto Juan Córdova. Aquella casa que vites allí con [dos pisos]. Nomás que la sala ya la tiraron. Patrás estaba la sala. Una sala larga. ¡Y grande! Y, tenían de estos faroles, lámparas de gaselín. Nomás se empezaban apagar, iban y le pompiaban, y agarraban gas. Y al último, ya ora después, el dijunto Porfirio Romero tenía una sala tamién.

Aá no se sentaban hombres. Nomás las puras mujeres. Los hombres estaban apartes. Los hombres estaban apartes. En ese tiempo no se costumbraba que un hombre iba a sentarse con una mujer aá. Güeno, tal vez sus maridos, pero casi ni sus maridos. Las mujeres estaban apartes, aá. Y ai iban a sacalas a bailar.

En ese tiempo no había cantinas, pero hacían mula. Y de ai era onde se emborrachaban. Pero en esos tiempos no había hombres, no había personas que

thing. That's what people were accustomed to long ago. But nobody killed anyone. People were different then, but that was people's way of life.

The ranches were scattered, far apart, and people came from all over. From all the ranches, and they gathered there in Guadalupe. At the church where mass was held. At night.

They wore only their pants, hat, and so forth. Ah, as for the women, another style was in vogue. Women didn't wear pants in those days. That was not fashionable then. Dresses, yes. Long hair . . . long suits were also fashionable.

Oh, the dances, no sooner had the sun gone down, once it got dark, they lasted. There were times that they lasted until three, four o'clock in the early morning. Oh yes! There was no end to them.

The one who had a dance hall, and he also had a store, was the late Juan Córdova. That house you saw [on a visit in 1985] with two stories. Except that the dance hall has already been torn down. The dance hall was toward the back. It was long. And large! And they had these lanterns, gas lamps. As soon as they started to go out, people would go and pump them up, and they got more gas. Toward the end, afterwards, the late Porfirio Romero also had a dance hall.

Over there men wouldn't sit down. Only the women. The men were alone. The men were by themselves. Back then it wasn't customary for a man to go sit down with the women. Okay, perhaps their husbands, but not even their husbands. The women were all alone, by themselves. And that's where men went to take them out to dance.

Back in those days there weren't any bars, but they made moonshine. And that's how they got drunk. But

jueran, que estuvieran alcojólicos. Cuando tocaba que hacían bailes, se embolaban, pero pasó, pasó . . . si peliaban, si se golpiaban, se daban con las cuartas, pero no se navajiaban. A golpes, a garrotazos, pero todo lo más al cuartazo (risas).

Pus andaban a caballo. Ai traiban las cuartas y cuando había tomulto, pos iban aá a las sillas, y agarraban la cuarta. Oh, yo llegué a ver una pelea que éste su papá de Damiano le pegó a un hombre, y era muy grandote él. Se peleó con él y luego . . . el dijunto Germán le pegó. Y era un hombre grandote . . . le pegó algo. No muncho. Loo los apartaron aí.

back then you didn't have men, you didn't have people who were, who were alcoholics. Whenever they had a dance, they'd get drunk, but it would come and go . . . if they fought, if they hit each other, it was with their quirts, but no knifings. Only with fists, blows, but everything else just quirt whippings (laughter).

They rode horseback to the dances. That's where they had their quirts, and so whenever there was a scuffle, well, they went to the saddles and they grabbed their quirts. Oh, I got to see this fight where Damiano's father whipped this man, and he [the father] was a huge man. He got into a fight with him and then . . . the late Germán beat him up. He was a huge man . . . he beat him up pretty good. Not much. Then they pulled them apart.

Nasario P. García. First Holy Communion, c. 1921.
Courtesy of Teodorita García-Ruelas.

18 DE OCTUBRE DE 1979
La Semana Santa

Güeno, la Semana Santa lo que, miércoles, güeno, yo
no sé el miércoles, pero jueves y viernes y sábado. El
jueves sacaban las Estaciones. El viernes tamién. Y el
sábado en la mañana cantaban gloria.

Salían de la iglesia al rumbo del campo santo.
Cuando ya llegaban a la mitá de las estaciones, ai
daban la güelta. Cuando ya acababan con la última
estación, ya estaban aí cerca del oratorio. Ves, pus aí
te van diciendo en las estaciones, cuando te tienes que
hincar y todo eso. Y luego que acaban ése, que rezan,

OCTOBER 18, 1979
Holy Week

Well, as far as Holy Week, Wednesday, well, I don't
know about Wednesday, but Thursday and Friday and
Saturday, yes. On Thursday they celebrated the
Stations of the Cross. Friday also. And on Saturday
morning they sang the gloria.

They'd leave the church headed for the cemetery.
When they were half through with the Stations of the
Cross, they'd turn around. When they finished with
the last station, they'd be back close to the oratory.

You see. Meantime you were told as you went along
reciting the Stations of the Cross, when you had to
kneel down and all of that sort of thing. And as soon as

Nasario García. First Holy Communion, c. 1944.

caminan un trecho como de aquí allá y luego vuelven con lotra estación . . . a mí se me hace que son doce [hay catorce].

Pues, ése era lo que, ése era lo que festejaban en tiempo santo los hermanos. No el padre. Los hermanos, porque, pus había como cinco o seis. Eran Ricardo [Tafoya], en primo Nicanor [Aragón] y munchos otros. No me acuerdo de los otros. De allí mesmo. [Pertenecían] a una morada que tenía Ricardo Tafoya. El oratorio, que le decían.

Decían pero yo no, yo no llegué a ver. Pero reclaman que eso lo hacían [darse azotes], como oculto. No en público. Porque se encerraban. Sí. En tiempo santo, como un día como el viernes o el jueves, les llevaban

they finished praying, they'd walk a stretch like from here to there [about 20 feet], and they'd recite the next station . . . I believe there are twelve of them [there are fourteen].

Well, that's what, that's what the Penitente Brothers celebrated during the holy period. Not the priest. The Penitente Brothers, because, well, there were about five or six of them. Yes, why there was Ricardo Tafoya, "Cousin" Nicanor Aragón, and many others. I don't remember the others, from right there in Guadalupe. They belonged to a morada that Ricardo Tafoya had, there in the oratory, as it was called.

People would say that they flagellated themselves, but I never, but I never got to see it. But people claim

comida aá el oratorio. Ellos no salían. Tenían que salir al escusao, yo no digo que no. No tenían escusao aá dentro (risas). Pero les llevaban comida. Aí se estaban encerraos.

they did that, like in secret. Not in public. Because they used to lock themselves up. Yes. During Lent, like on a Friday or Thursday, and people would take them food to the oratory. They wouldn't come outside. They had to come out to go to the outhouse, I don't deny that. They didn't have a restroom inside (laughter). But people took them food. They'd stay locked up in there.

18 DE OCTUBRE DE 1979
La Virgen

Güeno, pus cuando sacaban la Virgen tenían costumbre, el mayordomo, lo que era mayordomos, de sacar la Virgen, como era en el verano, ¿ves? Y ir casa por casa. Y con, en la última casa, que llegaban, que ya se estaba haciendo tarde, ai la dejaban. Pero ai la velaban. Le hacían velorio. Y otro día venían y seguían. Ése es cuando sacaban la Virgen.

Güeno, salían, salían de aquí de Gualupe, eh, iban por onde vivía el dijunto Martín, y luego aá por a case los Armijos, y loo de ai volvían por lotro lao del río [el Río Puerco], y, y se venían por de este lao del río hasta la última casa. Era de los Jaramillos. Y loo cruzaban paquel lao del río. Y agarraban las casas del dijunto Crescencio [Salas], las otras que estaban, y de ai llegaban a la iglesia, patrás [en la Placita].

Se remudaban. Mujeres y hombres tamién. Pero casi todo lo demás las mujeres cargaban la Virgen. La que era, casi siempre, las rezadoras, en ese tiempo cuando la Virgen, mi comadre Adelita [Gonzales], y ésta, ¿cómo se llama?, Griavelita [Salas]. Oh mi comadre Adelita era una rezadora que ésa a velorios y todo. Y Griavelita tamién.

The Virgin

Okay, well, whenever they took out the Virgin in a procession, they had the custom of, that is, the mayordomo, the mayordomos, of taking out the Virgin, like now in the summer, you see? And going from house to house. And with, and when they got to the last house, when it was getting late, that's where they left Her overnight. That's where they watched Her. That's where they had a vigil for Her. And next day people returned and they continued on with the procession. That's when they used to take out the Virgin.

Okay, people left, left from here in Guadalupe, eh, they'd go by where the late Martín used to live, and then over by the Armijos' house, and then from there they would return on the other side of the river [the Río Puerco], and then they'd return on this side of the river until they came to the last house. It was the Jaramillos'. And then they'd cross over to the other side of the river and they'd stop by the late Crescencio's [Salas] house, at the other houses also, and from there they got back to the church [in La Placita].

People took turns. Both men and women. But most of the time the women carried the Virgin. The one who was, almost always, the one who prayed, at that time when the Virgin was taken out, was my comadre Adelita [Gonzales], and what's here name? Griavelita [Salas]. Oh, my comadre Adelita was the person who prayed at vigils and all. And Griavelita also.

Nasario P. García's sisters, Teodorita and Julianita García, dressed as Comanches at Christmas, c. 1918. Courtesy of Teodorita García-Ruelas.

18 DE OCTUBRE DE 1979
Los Crismes

Pues, aá el rancho, que yo supiera, aá no se costumbraba de . . . cada quien, en su casa, pues festejaban los Crismes. Las casas estaban murre lejos pa que estuvieran pidiendo crismes. Pero lo que hacían a las doce de la noche, o en la madrugada, güeno, munchos, velaban al Niño. ¿Entiendes?

Y munchas veces se juntaban como es aá en el oratorio, o en la iglesia. Y luego a las cuatro de la mañana antonces cantaban, cantaban la alba. Y munchos lo hacían en sus casas. Velaban al Niño. Le rezaban, con toda la familia, a las cuatro de la mañana.

OCTOBER 18, 1979
Christmas

Well, over at the ranch, as far as I knew, we were not accustomed to . . . everyone, in their own homes celebrated Christmas. The houses were very far apart to go around asking for Christmas goodies. But what people did at twelve o'clock midnight, or early in the morning, well, many people held a vigil for the Baby Jesus. Understand? And many times they would gather like there in the oratory, or in the church. And then at four o'clock in the morning, then they sang, then they would sing the alba [morning song of praise]. Many people performed this ritual in their homes. They'd

Cuando ya venía el lucero, cantaban la alba. Mamá era muy güena pa eso. Yo me acuerdo. Estaba chiquito. Sí, la alba. Eso que dice, "Ai viene la alba con la luz del día." Oh, ¡muy bonito!

Empezaban y luego cuando ya nació el Niño. Pero la gente era muy religiosa en ese tiempo. Ya ora no. Ya ora puro *good time* y es verdá, no va uno ni a misa. Allá no, oye. En el rancho la gente, muy católica, muy religiosa. Onque juera en sus casas pero ellos adoraban a Dios, al Niño, cuando venían sus días y tal vez por eso mi Tata Dios nos ayudaba.

Como te digo, las casas, los ranchos, estaban muy retiraos. Pa los Crismes, me acuerdo yo, iba mamá y llenaba medias con dulces y loo las ponía y cuando nos levantábanos, pus nos decían que era del Santo Clos. ¡No Santo Clos! (risas).

Ora si iba uno a pedir crismes en algunas casas, le daban pasteles, bizcochos o dulces. Ése era todo. Más antes no se costumbraba el presente. ¡No!

hold a vigil for the Baby Jesus. People prayed to Him, along with each individual family, at four o'clock in the morning. When the morning star was about to make an appearance, they sang the alba. Mom was very good at that. I remember. I was very small. Yes, the alba. It goes something like this: "There comes the dawn with the light of day." Oh, it was very pretty!

They would start the ritual and then [again] when the Baby Jesus was born. But people were very religious back in those days. Yes. Now, not so. Now it's nothing but a good time, and it's true, people don't even go to mass anymore. Listen, not so over there. At the ranch, people were very Catholic, very religious, even if it was at home. But people prayed to God, to the Baby Jesus, when their holy days came, and perhaps that's the reason my Fatherly God helped us.

As I'm telling you, the houses, the ranches, were very far apart from each other. For Christmas, I remember, Mom would go and fill up the stockings with candy, and she'd hang them up and when we woke up, she'd tell us they were from Santa Claus. No such thing as Santa Claus! (laughter).

Now if you went to ask for Christmas goodies at some of the homes, they gave you pies, bizcochitos, or candy. That's all. Long ago it was not customary to give presents. No sir!

18 DE OCTUBRE DE 1979
Un entierro

No, pus, eh, [cuando moría alguien], los velaban. Todas las gentes se juntaban y salían a avisar a las gentes por los ranchos. No como ora. Se muere alguien y lo ponen en el papel; ya cuando uno sabe lo han enterrao. Antonces no. De una vez sabía uno por un rumbo y otro por otro. Se muría alguien y iban a la iglesia y empezaban a doblar y ya nomás se oía, se oía de muy lejos, ya sabían quién se muriría. Pos loo van a la novedá. Y loo unos pescaban por un rumbo y otros por otros, avisándole[s] a todos que se murió tal persona. Y se juntaba la gente al velorio y al entierro.

Ricardo Tafoya era uno de los que hacía cajones. Venían aquí, despachaban aquí, a la Plaza, o el lugar más cerca, paque trujiera de esa garra negra y blanca paceles crucitas. Sí. Ése era todo. No les ponían . . . el puro cajón nomás. No había sobre cajón, ni nada. Yo creo que ya cuando acababan de echale la tierra, ya estaba desbaratao el cajón. Pus onde iba a soportar el cajón. Pero asina los enterraban.

Me acuerdo yo que en una vez, yo no sé a quién lo llevaron en carro de caballos. Y pienso que asina lo llevaban, en un carro de caballos, hasta el campo santo.

Todos iban. ¡Todos iban! Algunas veces los dolientes, algunos, se quedarían aá en la casa. Pero casi todos iban.

OCTOBER 18, 1979
A Burial

No, well, ah, [whenever anyone died], they held a vigil
for them. All the people got together and they went out
and notified the other people in the ranches. Not like
now. If someone dies all they do is put their name in
the newspaper. By the time you find out about it,
they've buried the deceased. Not so then. Right away
you knew from one end of the village to the other. If
someone died, someone went to the church and started
to toll the bells, and once you heard the bells, one
could hear them from far away, people knew someone
had died. People right away went to find out what was
going on. And some took off in one direction and
others in another, notifying people that so and so had
died. Then people got together for the vigil and the burial.

Ricardo Tafoya was one of the ones who made
coffins. People came here, they'd send someone to
Albuquerque, or to the closest place, so he could bring
some of that black and white gauze to cut out little
crosses for the coffin. Yes. That's all. They didn't have
anything but the coffin itself. There wasn't an outer
coffin or anything. I believe that by the time they
finished pouring the sand on top of the coffin, it was
already in several pieces. How could the coffin possibly
support the weight [of the dirt]? But that's the way they
buried people.

I remember one time, don't know who it was, but
they took him by horse wagon. I believe that's the way
they took them, by horse wagon, to the cemetery.

Everybody went. Everyone! At times the bereaved,
some, not all, would probably stay at home. But just
about everyone went to the burial.

Una partera

Güeno, eh, cada quien . . . tenía, eh, yo creo, cada partera tenía su idea. No te poo esplicar pero les daban [a las mujeres que iban a tener niño] jumazos, con diferentes remedios. Y asina las tenían hasta que nacía la criatura. Yo me acuerdo que les daban jumazos en un cajete. Y cosas asina, ¿ves? No te poo decir qué hierbas usarían ellas. Echaban [las parteras] en alguna cosa brasas y loo le echaban esto y lotro y ai se sentaban y hacía jumo. Eso les daban asegún entiendo yo pa que, pa que la mujer se abreviara. Y una partera tenía que tener una ayudanza.

Pues, eh, yo creo que tenía que estar [la mujer], que me acuerdo yo, no menos que diez días. De cinco a diez días [en la cama después de nacer el bebé]. Oh no, ¡cuarenta días!

En esos tiempos creo que cobraban [las parteras] diez pesos.

A Midwife

Well, ah, everyone . . . had, ah, I believe, each midwife had her own ways. I can't explain it, but the midwives did apply fumigations, with different remedies. And that's what they did [with prospective mothers], until the child was born. I remember that they'd give fumigations in a tin tub. And things like that, do you understand? I can't tell you what herbs they would use. The midwives would put embers into something and then they'd put this or that and then they sat there and smoke came out. The midwives did that as I understand, so that, to speed up birth. And the midwife had to have an assistant.

Well, ah, I believe that the woman [the new mother] had to stay in bed after birth, as far as I can remember, no less than ten days. From five to ten days. Oh no, forty days!

Back in those days I believe they charged ten dollars [to deliver a child].

Perfilia Córdova, folk healer, and Tomasita, a friend, c. 1909.
Courtesy of Teodorita García-Ruelas.

18 DE OCTUBRE DE 1979
Las curanderas

Pues que me acuerde yo, la dijunta Utimia. Utimia.
¿De qué era? Leyba, pienso. Ésa era una de las más
viejas, de las primeras curanderas. Y luego ya al último,
oh, la dijunta Gavina, oye. ¿Sabes quién es la dijunta
Gavina? Sánchez . . . Ésa era una las más viejas
curanderas que había ai en Gualupe.

Yo creo que, como ora pa enfermedades y todo eso,
ellas no usaban más de remedios mexicanos, yerbas.
Diferentes clases de yerbas, como es yerba güena y
munchos remedios mexicanos. Hasta con la yerba de la
vívora y todo eso curaban.

OCTOBER 18, 1979
Folk Healers

Well, as far as I can remember, the late Utimia. Utimia.
What was her last name? Leyba, I believe. She was one
of the oldest, one of the first folk healers. And toward
the end, oh, the late Gavina, hear? Do you know who
the late Gavina is? Sánchez . . . She was one of the
oldest folk healers there was in Guadalupe.

I believe that, like now for illnesses and all of that,
all they did was to use Mexican remedies. Plants.
Different kinds of plants, like for example, mint, and
many Mexican remedies. They even treated people like
with snakeweed and all of that kind of thing.

Pus, la yerba de la vívora, pues, pa munchas cosas [se usaba]. Les daban baños. Ora si estaban resfriaos o alguna cosa, o que se sintieran mal, pos munchas veces les daban baños con yerba de la vívora. Usaban trementina.

Pues yo creo que sí [creían en el mal ojo]; en esos tiempos sí. Ahora en estos tiempos no creiban, pero más antes sí. [Para curar] pus buscaban un juan, que lo escupiera [al niño]. O corretiaban un juan, onde hubiera, pa que lo curaran cuando les hacían ojo.

[Y] pus cuando estaban [algunos] solevaos, pus las curanderas les metían el dedo (risas).

Cuando estaban empachaos, cuando estaban empachaos, le andaban con un güevo. Cuando se reventaba el güevo, ai . . . (risas).

Well, snakeweed, well, it was good to heal many things. It was good in baths. For example if you had a cold or something like that. Or if you felt bad, many times they just bathed you in a snakeweed solution.

They also used turpentine. Well I believe so [they believed in the evil eye]; back in those days I believe they did. Nowadays they may not believe in it, but back then they did, yes. In order to cure it [the evil eye], well, they looked for a Juan [in the family] so he could spit on the child. Or they tracked a Juan down wherever it was so he could cure the child whenever somebody cast the evil eye spell on it.

Now, when people were suffering from shock, well the folk healers simply put their finger up their rectum [to insert a suppository] (laughter).

When someone [a child] was constipated, when they were constipated, the folk healers used an egg. When the egg cracked, that was it! (laughter).

Resfríos

Pa resfríos, si una persona estaba resfriada, pues, eh, lo
que hacían era aflotalo con, eh, güeno lo flotaban con
. . . mejor dijirte, si una persona estaba resfriada, lo
curaban con agua de, le daban a beber de esta agua de
caramelo. Y si tenían muncho descalofrío, batían
güevo y le echaban, le echaban ya juera poleo, más bien
poleo, y le ponían parches en la planta de los pies. Pus
nomás jirvían la azúcar y lo hacían que se hiciera
caramelo, ¿ves? Y loo se lo daban a beber. Ése es pa
que le sacaran la fiebre.

MARCH 30, 1982
Colds

For colds, if a person had a cold, well, ah, what was done was to rub the person down with, ah, well they rubbed the person with . . . let me put it this way. If a person had a cold, they'd treat him or her with water diluted with, they'd give the person what was called caramel water to drink. And if the person had a lot of chills, they'd beat an egg and they mixed it, whether it was with peppermint, more than likely peppermint, and they'd put patches on the bottom of the patient's feet. Well, all they had to do to make the caramel was to boil the sugar until it turned into caramel, understand? Then they'd give it to the patient to drink. The purpose was to draw out the fever.

El aigre

Pues, eh, yo no estoy muy cierto, pero a lo que sé yo, que muncha gente les daba aigre, que y munchas veces se sentaban cerca de una ventana, o cerca de una puerta. Y ai era onde les daba aigre. Y el aigre les pegaba ya juera, les podía pegar en un ojo; les podía pegar en un sentido.

Pues, eh, yo no sé en los ojos, pero en los sentidos sí sé yo que, que buscaban la nuez. Le echaban nuez en un algodoncito y se lo ponía, porque cuando tenía aigre en el sentido les repicaba muncho y loo no oían muy bien. Y con la nuez, puesto ai, por algunos días, se les quitaba.

Drafts

Well, ah, I'm not very sure, but based on what I know,
a lot of people suffered from drafts, because many
times they'd sit close to a window, or close to a door.
And that's how they suffered from drafts. And a draft
could hit them whether . . . it could strike an eye; it
could strike an ear.

Well, ah, I don't know about the eyes, but as far as
the ears I do know that, that people looked for nutmeg.
People would put nutmeg on a small piece of cotton
and they'd apply it, because when a person suffered
from a draft in the ears, they'd ring a lot, and then
people couldn't hear very well. And with nutmeg
applied to the ears, for a few days, it would go away.

30 DE MARZO DE 1982
Una solevada

Oh sí, más antes eso sí creiban. Los dotores toavía ora mismo no saben; no creyen. Pero ése es una cosa que costumbraba, que tenían por esperencia más antes—solevar. Y una persona que, eh, se soleva, que se está muncho tiempo, se puede morir.

Pues una solevada puede pegar de susto, de gusto, o de un golpe, y cosas asina.

Si una persona no tiene nada y, y se asusta, se soleva. Un golpe también, que pegue un golpe en esta parte aquí, como es decir en la cadera, se puede solevar.

A Slight Case of Shock

Oh, yes, they believed in that, alright. Even today the doctors don't know; they don't believe in it. But that's one thing that used to happen, that people experienced long ago, which was to suffer a slight case of shock. And a person who, ah, suffers from shock, that experience stays with the person for a long time, and he or she can die.

Well, a slight case of shock can come as a result of fright, from excitement, or as a result of a blow, and things like that.

If there's nothing wrong with a person and, and they get frightened, they suffer from slight shock. A blow does the same thing; for example, if a person receives a blow like in this area, that's to say, the hip, they can suffer shock.

30 DE MARZO DE 1982
Enyerbao

[Una] enyerbada quería decir que, como enbrujao. Pues, eh, eh, ése era lo que . . . ése está enyerbao. Era que alguna brujería le había hecho.

Oh sí, [se ponía malo] mayormente si tomaba licor; se podía volver loco. Aquí estaba, por ejemplo, te voy a decir, en primo, ¿cómo se llamaba?, Juan Sandoval. Reclamaban que le habían hecho mal, la misma cosa que, que lo tenían enyerbao. Ésa es la palabra. ¡Brujerías! Ese hombre, nomás tomaba un trago y se volvía loco. Oh, pus quería acabar con todo. Quería acabar con la casa y todo.

Tenían que buscar una, una persona curandera, que supiera. Y ésas curaban nomás con remedios mexicanos. Tenían que saber; tenían que saber. Eso no todos lo pueden hacer.

Bewitched

A person who was *enyerbada* meant that they were like bewitched. Well, ah, ah, that's what . . . that man's *enyerbao*, bewitched. It's just that someone had cast a spell on him.

Oh yes, a person got really sick, especially if he drank liquor; he could go crazy. There was, for example, I'm going to tell you, cousin, what's his name? Juan Sandoval. People claimed that someone had bewitched him, the same thing as, being *enyerbao*. That's the word. Witchcraft. That man, the moment he took a drink of liquor, he went crazy. Oh, why he wanted to destroy everything. He wanted to put an end to the house and all.

[To cure this illness] they had to look for a, a person who was a folk healer, who knew about that stuff. And those folk healers would treat the patients using only Mexican remedies. Folk healers had to know; they had to know. Not everyone knows about that sort of thing.

30 DE MARZO DE 1982
Se les cae la mollera

Oh sí, sí, eso, eso la curaban muncho. Los dotores ora no saben nada.

Pues, eh, reclamaban que cuando está, es decir, un niño, un *baby* muy chiquito, dígase que le den teta o que le den chiche, munchas veces, si le sacan, como, muy recio la teta, se les cae la mollera porque se la bajan por aquí, ¿ves?

Con un vaso con agua, asina [la levantaban], y loo se la iban levantando parriba, parriba, y loo les metían el dedo acá [en el paladar], parriba, y la iba levantando. El *pressure* del agua iba llevando el . . . [la mollera].

MARCH 30, 1982
The Fontanel Falls

Oh yes, yes, that sort of thing, that sort of thing was treated a lot. The doctors nowadays don't know anything about it.

Well, ah, people claimed that when a child is, that is to say, when a baby is very small. Let us say that they bottle-feed it or breast-feed it, a lot of times, if they like, jerk out the nipple, the fontanel falls because it drops right here [the top of the head], you see?

With a glass of water, that's how [they would raise it]. The fontanel was raised little by little upwards, upwards, and then they'd put a finger here [on the child's palate], upwards, and the fontanel went up and up. The pressure from the water kept raising the [fontanel].

El empacho

Oh sí. Oh sí. Güeno, pus, eh, eh, [los niños] se
empachaban de, podían comer alguna cosa que les
hacía mal. Les pegaba en el estógamo.

Sí, pus masa cruda se les pega y, y como curaban el
empacho, con un güevo. Le andaban aquí [en el
estómago] con un güevo. Que te daban un gücvo, y lo
detenían aquí. Cuando se reventaba, onde se reventaba
el güevo, onde se reventaba el güevo, ai sabían que
estaba empachao. Y tamién, eh, loo los volteaban pa
bajo y les jalaban, les jalaban un cuero en el espinazo
pa que se les quitara el empacho.

JULY 1991
Indigestion

Oh yes. Oh yes. Okay, well, ah, children got indigestion from, from eating something that made them ill. It would hit them in the stomach.

Yes, well raw dough gets stuck to their intestines and, and the way they cured indigestion was with an egg. They'd rub here [the child's stomach] with an egg; they'd hold it here. When the egg broke, where the egg broke, where the egg broke, they knew that was the spot where the indigestion was centered. And, ah, they'd also . . . and then they'd turn them over on their stomach and they'd pull their skin; they'd pull their skin on their back so they'd get rid of the indigestion.

El mal ojo

Oh sí, sí. La gente de más antes ellos creiban muncho
en eso. El, ah, en esto de hacer ojo no todas las
personas podían, tenían su, su, ¿cómo?, su persona pa
ser, pa ser ojo. Por ejemplo, había personas, de las
personas que hacían ojo. Dígase que vieran un
chiquito, y les gustaba muncho. Ellos no sabían. Le
llamaban la atención; le hacían ojo. Munchas veces no
sabían ni quién. Munchas veces munchos sí sabían
que hacían ojo porque le daba dolor de cabeza o bascas
o alguna cosa. Ai sabían que ellos habían hecho ojo.

A lo que sé yo, eh, pues tenían que buscar a la
persona que consideraban que le hacían ojo y los
llevaban a que los escupieran. Nomás los escupían y, y,
se les quitaba.

Y otras personas que podían curar el ojo era, no
importaba que esta persona no le hiciera ojo a un
chiquito o lo que juera, un Juan. Un Juan. Correteaban
muncho a los Juanes pa que, pa que curaran el ojo.

JULY 1981
The Evil Eye

Oh yes, yes. The people of yesteryear, they believed a lot in that sort of thing. The, ah, in the business of casting an evil eye. Not everyone could do it. They had their, their, how should I say? They had their, it was in them to cast, to cast an evil eye. For example, there were people who, who would cast the evil eye. Let us say that they would see a child, and they admired him a lot. They didn't know. The child would be attracted to them; they cast the evil eye. Many times people didn't even know who the culprit was. Many times many people suspected that a child had the evil eye, because it was suffering from headaches or vomiting or something. That's how they knew that someone had cast the evil eye.

As far as what I know, ah, they had to look for the person who they thought had cast the evil eye, so they would spit in the child's face. All they had to do was to spit on the child and, and, the evil eye was gone.

And other persons who could cure the evil eye were, and it didn't matter if the persons themselves had not cast the evil eye on the child or whatever, a Juan. A Juan. People used to track down the Juans a lot, so that they, so that they could cure the evil eye.

Dos brujas y dos Juanes

Mi agüelo se llamaba Juan García, su papá de en papá, y estaba cieguito. Y él venía de allá de Gualupe pacá pa la Plaza, pa Alburquerque. Y no sé con quién vendría él, o a qué vendría. Yo no sé si a llevar provisiones. Yo no sé, pero ai en la Ceja, onde estaban campeando—era en el mes de mayo—vieron, vieron venir dos luces. Iban de aquí de Alburquerque. Y loo empezaron a platicar él y sus otros compañeros, y venía *otro* Juan tamién, amás de mi agüelo. Y loo es que les preguntó mi agüelo que si de qué rumbo venían las luces. Ya le dijieron. "Pues, llévame," es que le dijo mi agüelo a en papá, y se jueron los dos Juanes, lejos de dionde tenían el campo. Ai es que hicieron una raya los Juanes pal rumbo que venían las dos luces. Hicieron una raya con una rueda, una aquí y otra allá, una pa cada luz. Loo se quitaron, sí, se quitaron, la camiseta y la pusieron en cada rueda y se jueron patrás pal campo. Cuando de güenas a primeras aquí van las luces y se desparecieron. Al rato vinieron mi agüelo y el otro Juan a ver y es que ai estaban cobijadas dos mujeres con las camisetas que dejaron los Juanes.

Tengo entendido que éstas eran dos mujeres que iban pa la Sierra del Valle, que le llaman, par onde estaban sus maridos en la borrega, tresquilando. Es que las mujeres eran de aquí de Los Duranes o de Los Griegos en Alburquerque; o no sé diónde dijo en papá. Eso sí me platicaba en papá.

¡Pues eran brujas! ¡Brujas! ¡Qué pueden haber sido! Estas brujas iban volando, ¿ves?, pero aquéllos, los Juanes, pueden agarrar las brujas, si saben. ¿Entiendes?

OCTOBER 18, 1979
Two Witches and Two Juans

My paternal grandfather's name was Juan García, and he was blind. He was on his way from Guadalupe to town, to Albuquerque. I don't know who he could have been coming with, or the purpose of the trip. I don't know if it was to take groceries back to the ranch. I just don't know, but there in La Ceja, where they were camping—it was during the month of May—they saw two lights coming. The lights were headed from here in Albuquerque. And then he and his other buddies began to talk. In addition, there was another Juan, besides my grandfather. And then I understand my grandfather asked them which direction the lights were coming from, so they told him. "Well, take me," my grandfather supposedly said to my dad, and the two fellows named John took off, far from where their camp was. There they made a line in the direction of the lights. They made a line with a circle, one in one place and another in another, one for each light. Then each Juan took off, yes, each one took off his undershirt and put it in each circle, and returned to the campsite When all of a sudden, here go the lights; they disappeared. A little while later my grandfather and the other fellow named John returned to see, and there were two women covered with the two undershirts that my grandfather and the other Juan had left.

I understand that these two women were on their way to La Sierra del Valle, as it's called, where their husbands were shearing sheep. The women supposedly were from Los Duranes or Los Griegos in Albuquerque; or I don't know where my dad said they were from. Yeah, that's what my dad used to tell me.

Los Juanes tienen muncho poder, si saben pa agarrar las brujas. Tocó que en esa oportunidá había dos Juanes.

Pues, eh, es que ellas les dijieron a ellos que iban pa la Sierra del Valle, par onde estaban sus maridos, que estaban en la tresquila. Antonces ellas les ofrecían no sé qué tantas cabras nomás porque las soltaran. Las soltaron. Y se levantaron ellas y se jueron. Volando. Pero reclaman, yo no sé en qué modo lo harán, que pueden salir pa juera y ai mesmo pueden volverse como un pájaro y volar. Eso sí me platicaba en papá.

Well, they were witches! Witches! What else could they have been! These witches were airborne, you see, but those fellows named John, they're capable of catching them, provided they know how. Do you understand? The Juans have a lot of power, if they know how to catch witches. It so happened that on that occasion there were two Juans.

Well the women presumably told them that they were headed for La Sierra del Valle, where their husbands were, who were involved in shearing sheep. When the witches offered the two Juans I don't know how many goats, if they would just turn them loose. They did so. And they rose and took off. Flying. But people claim that the witches are able to go outside, and right there they can turn into a bird and fly. I don't know how they manage it. Yeah, that's what my dad used to tell me.

18 DE OCTUBRE DE 1979
Un mono

Te voy a contar lo que en papá me platicaba. Posible que él estuviera joven toavía. Yo no estaba nacido en ese tiempo. Güeno, el cuento es que en papá me platicaba que él y sus amigos iban a los bailes en Salazar. Era, en ese tiempo, muy mentao. Hacían munchos bailes en ese lugar.

Había un hombre; él tocaba el violín. Y una noche venía de Salazar. No sé si vendría en un burro o en una mula, pero no era caballo. Ai en un lugar que le dicen el Alto de los Jaramillos, ai venía este hombre solo. Cuando llegó en el Alto ese, es que salió uno, como un mono, y se le subió en las anancas. El hombre se asustó muncho. El cuento es que cuando llegó a la casa, que, que, que vido la luz, se desmayó.

En ese Alto de los Jaramillos, según platicaba en papá, que es que ai salían munchas cosas. Eh, no brujas, pero como bultos y cosas asina.

A Rag Doll

I'm going to tell you what my dad used to talk to me about. It's possible that he was still very young. I wasn't born yet. Well, the fact is that my dad used to tell me that he and friends of his would go to dances in Salazar. Back in those days, Salazar was well-known. They held many dances in that village.

There was a man, he played the violin, and one night he was on his way back from Salazar. I'm not sure whether he was riding a donkey or a mule, but it wasn't a horse. At a place called El Alto de los Jaramillos, here came this man riding all alone. When he got to El Alto, someone emerged, like a rag doll, and it climbed on the donkey's rump. The man got terribly frightened. The fact is that when he got home, when he, he, he saw the kitchen light, he fainted.

On that Alto de los Jaramillos, according to what my dad talked about, many things supposedly appeared. Ah, not witches, but like shapes, things like that.

Galo García, Guadalupe, c. 1942.

18 DE OCTUBRE DE 1979
Apareció un caballo

Y tamién es que venían una vez como dos o tres hombres, y éstos traiban sus güenos caballos y todo. Seguro que venían embolaos. De todos modos, me platicaba en papá que cuando iban por El Alto ese de los Jaramillos, es que ai se les apareció un caballo adelante de ellos. Loo es que dijo uno de ellos: "¿Y este caballo de diónde resultó?" es que les dijo. Pronto sacó su cabresto, lo amarró en la cabeza de la silla y es que gritó: "Yo lo lazo." Y le partió pero salió a juir el caballo. Pos lo alcanzó y lo lazó. Cuando los

OCTOBER 18, 1979
A Horse Appeared

Another time I understand there were about two or three men, and they were riding their best horses and everything. For sure they were drunk. Anyhow, my dad told me that when these men were crossing El Alto, named after the Jaramillos, a horse appeared out of nowhere in front of them. Then one of them I guess said: "And where in the world did this horse come from?" so he said. In a flash he took out his rope, tied it to the saddle horn, and hollered: "I'll rope it." And he took off after it, but the horse took off running. Well, he caught up with it and roped it. When his

compañeros llegaron, él estaba caido par un lao y su caballo pal otro y el cabresto en el suelo, pero el caballo que había lazao no estaba.

Eso me platicaba en papá de los Moras. Asina se llamaban ellos; eran los Moras.

friends got there, he was on one side and his horse on the other and the rope on the ground, but the horse he had roped was nowhere in sight.

That's what my dad used to tell me about the Moras. That was their name, the Moras.

Un bulto

Una vez en San Luis, pus, eh, yo iba ya tarde, como a las tres de la mañana; iba a pie, cuando estábanos trabajando ai en el WPA. Esa noche había una de estas juntas de políticos y se jueron todos y de ai me jui yo a pie. Cuando yo ya llegué, que pasé la plaza de San Luis, eh, vide venir un bulto negro. Aquí viene todo el camino. Antonces yo dije: "Quizás viene alguien." Antes de llegar, como de aquí allá a la puerta, a unos cuatro, cinco pies, empecé a hablale, pero este, este bulto no contestaba nada. Era un bulto todo negro y cruzó el camino y entró asina a un chamisal. Después que ya se dirigió asina a la izquierda al chamisal, pal rumbo de la mesa, pues antonces me dio miedo a mí. Luego se apartó pallá el bulto ese, pal rumbo de la mesa, y yo me jui todo el camino pal campo. Yo le hablé pero sabrá Dios quién, quién sería. Y todo lo que vide jue nomás un bulto negro de arriba hasta bajo, que me acuerdo yo. ¡Ya eran las tres de la mañana!

OCTOBER 18, 1979
A Dark Object

One time in San Luis, well, ah, it was already late, like
three o'clock in the morning, and I was on my way
home. I was on foot. That's when we were working for
the WPA. There had been one of those political
meetings that night, and everyone went, including
myself. On foot. By the time I arrived, as I passed the
village of San Luis, ah, I saw a black shape coming
toward me. Here it comes right down the road. Then I
said to myself: "I guess somone's coming." Before it got
to where I was, like from here to the door, about four
or five feet, I started to talk to it, but this shape
wouldn't answer. It was a completely black shape; it
crossed the road and went right into the sagebrush.
After going left toward the sagebrush, by way of the
mesa [infamous supernatural locale], then I got scared.
Then that dark shape took off that way, in the direction
of the mesa, and I took off down the road for the
campsite. I spoke to it, but God knows who, who it
was. And the only thing I saw was a black shape, from
head to toe, as far as I can recollect. It was already
three o'clock in the morning!

III
Confrontation with Reality, 1928–1944

Adulthood came early in the Río Puerco valley during the 1920s for young men like my father, sometimes years before their maturation had run its normal course. By the time my father reached his late teenage years, he had been transformed into a man; he had gone from the status of dependent adolescent to independent adult. Maturing at a tender age, becoming a man before his time, was the rule rather than the exception, due primarily to family economic needs on the ranch. My father's situation was rather typical and commonplace. Reality in his case had a headstart and simply ran faster than, and ahead of, the clock.

The first glimpse of this comes to light in "El Río de las Vacas," where my father, already a school dropout, turns cowboy at age sixteen (in 1928), in order to earn a few cents per day to help support the family. But in addition to the money, we see a young man accepting responsibilities, self-discipline, and team spirit in a cattle drive. A wrangler's life (*la vida de un vaquero*) was often spiced with a little moonshine or corn liquor, resulting in "Borracheras" ("Sprees"), testimony to the fact that temptation for alcohol and its psychological effects remain constant and unchanged regardless of who we are, and irrespective of the time period we live in.

A cowboy's life was made easier if he owned a good horse; it was often his only source of pride and joy. The story of "El caballo colorao" ("The Sorrel Horse") is the cowboy's dream of an ideal horse, a perfect companion, especially when it came to cattle roundups ("Entre todos juntaban las vacas"). This was the time to show off your best mount. The results were not always flattering, as we see in "Le sacó la silla la vaca" ("The Cow Pulled Off His Saddle"), an event that almost ended in disaster. And

tragedies did occur; "Se trozó la mano" ("He Cut Off His Hand") is indicative of such mishaps. A less drastic mishap is portrayed in "Un golpeo" ("A Drop Off"), where a truck plunges into an arroyo after the crossing has been washed away.

The ax murder of Juan Valdez in "La muerte de Juan Valdez" ("The Death of Juan Valdez") represents a shockingly different kind of tragedy. Violence on a lower scale and precipitated by different motives is witnessed in "El dijunto Sotero" ("The Late Sotero").

Bernardino Hovey, a close friend and political confidant of my grandfather Teodoro García, was extremely popular and well-liked in the Río Puerco valley. His natural instincts for leadership surface in "Perdió muncho la gente" ("The People Lost a Lot"), relating how he stood up to government officials for what he perceived to be injustices against ranchers, following the lockout (circa 1938) of their cattle from the Ojo del Espíritu Santo land grant, where they had pastured their cattle in the past. The government's "infringement," as they saw it, virtually ensured the starvation of their cattle, but thanks to Bernardino Hovey's courage and tenacity, for which he was even jailed, the rangers and their entourage acquiesced and permitted limited grazing access to the Ojo del Espíritu Santo Grant. Despite Hovey's protests and the outcry from his followers, however, the people still emerged as losers, which is truly what began to drive people like my father out of the Río Puerco valley.

In 1933 my father departed for Bernalillo to work; that is where he met my mother. He was a janitor at the courthouse, a job obtained through my grandfather's political connections; my mother was a housekeeper at the Jesús Córdova household. They were married in 1935 at

the San Ignacio Church in Martíneztown in Albuquerque: he was twenty-two, she was sixteen. Immediately after the wedding, they moved to Guadalupe.

Here they lived with his parents until they were able to build a home of their own, next to my grandparents. My father, meantime, attempted to farm and raise cattle, but, because of the droughts, it was a doomed endeavor. The crops were meager, and the limited number of cattle that could be raised because of newly imposed government restrictions eventually sounded the death knell of most farmers and ranchers in the Río Puerco valley.

Government help and assistance through different agencies and programs only delayed the exodus and prolonged the agony of the people. After the Soil Conservation Service (SCS) was established in 1935, under the auspices of the United States Department of Agriculture, my father was employed by it, from 1936 to 1937, for forty-five cents per hour. The SCS was designed for projects to assist farmers and ranchers to maximize their water resources and land use by reducing flooding and soil erosion. My father also claims that he built fences, ironically enough, to protect government lands from ranchers like himself. From 1938 to 1939, he worked for the Works Progress Administration (WPA), later called the Works Projects Administration, also founded in 1935 as part of Franklin D. Roosevelt's New Deal. He built roads around Cabezón for about sixty cents per hour. In 1939 he returned to work for the SCS until 1944. At that time he was earning about sixty-five cents per hour.

While he was away during the week, my mother performed household chores, canned vegetables and fruits, fed the chickens and rabbits, chopped wood, and did other farm work normally earmarked for men. This became a standard routine, although my father was given summers

off from the SCS to plant and to work on the farm, until the agency ceased operations in the Río Puerco valley in 1944.

That summer he tried farming again, but without irrigation it was a futile effort; so shortly thereafter in 1944, he and my mother decided to move to Martineztown, in Albuquerque. There six of us lived in a one-room "dwelling" until we moved to Los Ranchos de Albuquerque, in 1948, where my father built a home.

The lack of pasturage for cattle, coupled with droughts, insufficient crops and a host of other setbacks, had sealed the fate of the Río Puerco valley ranchers and farmers. These were realities people faced squarely, having become accustomed to one misfortune or another during their lifetimes. In that sense my father and many of his compatriots experienced similar realities. At the same time, they recognized that in the end there were to be no winners, only losers, created by the forces of nature or regulations superimposed by the government such as soil conservation measures and limited grazing privileges.

All of the foregoing factors, and more, ultimately contributed to the economic strangulation of Río Puerco residents, for there is no substitute for food on the table or fodder in the fields. The imminent wholesale starvation of cattle loomed on the horizon for many Río Puerco valley residents such as my father. He, like others finally tucked their pride underneath the soles of their shoes and walked on it, as they abandoned their beloved valley, not knowing what fate awaited them beyond.

30 DE MARZO DE 1982
El Río de las Vacas

Yo tendría en ese tiempo, fíjate tú, como diez y seis años. Éste era, ese tiempo don Manuel Casaus jalaba las vacas pallá [para Cuba]. Era como en abril o el día quince de mayo. No, ya yo no estaba en la escuela en ese tiempo. Fácil tendría más de diez y seis, diez y siete años.

Y ai íbanos yo y Leonardo Trujillo a ayudale a Manuel. Íbanos los tres o cuatro o los que jueran por el atajo de vacas hasta que las subíanos a la Sierra, de aquí de Gualupe a la Sierra de Cuba. Manuel era el dueño. Nosotros éranos los trabajadores, nomás. Pues, él iba a invernar aá a Gualupe. Iba como en noviembre y en mayo las levantaba pa la Sierra.

Sí. Oh sí. Llevaban un campero. Llevaban un hombre en un carro de caballos con campo. Y, ah, salíanos en la mañana. Le figurábanos onde podíanos estar pa mediodía. Ai ya cuando llegábanos a mediodía, ai nos esperaba el campero con la comida y todo. Y luego no sé si eran cuatro o dos, detenían las vacas en lo que los dos comían y loo venían los otros y las detenían hasta que iban a comer los otros. Y los que venían, seguían.

Íbanos a la Sierra de Cuba, al Río de las Vacas, que le dicen. Al Río de las Vacas. Nos tardábanos dos días, muy bien. Dos días. Llevábanos como ochenta o cien [vacas].

Salíanos como de ai de Gualupe. Dígase que tuviéranos chanza de llegar a la Ventana. Figurábanos de llegar a un lugar onde hubiera corral, y ai las encerrábanos en un corral. O en un cerco, que hubiera,

MARCH 30, 1982
El Río de las Vacas

I must have been at that time, just imagine, about
sixteen years old. At that time Don Manuel Casaus
used to take the cattle there [to Cuba]. It was around
April or the fifteenth of May. I was no longer in school
at that time. Maybe I was sixteen, seventeen years old.

And there we were, Leonardo Trujillo and I, helping
Manuel. There we went, the three or four of us or
however many of us there were, after the herd of cows,
until we got them to La Sierra, from here in Guadalupe
to La Sierra de Cuba. Manuel was the owner of the
cattle. We were the workers; that's all. Well, he'd go
spend the winter there in Guadalupe. He'd go in
November, and in May he'd herd them back up to La
Sierra.

Yes. Oh yes. They had a *campero* [cook]. They had a
man on a horse wagon with the camping needs. And,
ah, we'd leave in the morning. We'd calculate where
we might be by noon. By the time we got to our
destination by noon, the *campero* would be waiting for
us with lunch and everything. And then I don't know if
it was four or two of us who watched the cows while
the other two ate, and then the others came and
watched the cows until the others went and ate. Those
who came followed suit.

We headed for La Sierra de Cuba, to a place called El
Río de las Vacas. El Río de las Vacas. We took every
bit of two days. Two days. We took about eighty or a
hundred cows.

We'd leave like from Guadalupe. Let's say we were
lucky enough to get to La Ventana. We'd figure on

porque él [don Manuel Casaus] siempre se aprevenía a
onde podía uno llegar, pa encerrar los animals en la
noche.

El campero llevaba la cama y todo de uno, ¿ves?
Pero uno llevaba sus caballos; llevaba dos caballos cada
uno. Naturalmente. Un día usaba uno y otro día otro.

Seis reales al día . . . cuando ya acababa uno. Cuando
ya acabábanos, salíanos de aquí. Dígase que nos
tardáranos dos días; llegábanos . . . al tercer día ya
estábanos arriba de la Sierra. O podríanos estarnos dos
días más, marcando, descornando o haciendo otra cosa
hasta que ya se desocupaba uno.

Cuando ya se desocupaba, nos llevaba este Manuel,
que era el patrón, pa Cuba, como en la tarde, que
juéranos a venir otro día. Aá en Cuba, allá teníanos
casa y too. Nos daba de comer y en la mañana nos
veníanos de aá de Cuba, en los caballos de nosotros.

Pos había oportunidá de ir a ganar alguna cosa y me
iba con él [Manuel Casaus]. En ese tiempo no había ni
onde ganar cuatro reales. Y si había onde ganar seis
reales, pus, aí se iba uno, porque no había onde.

getting to a place where there would be a corral. That's where we'd lock up the cattle. Or wherever there was a fence. Because Don Manuel Casaus always made plans for where we should go, to lock up the animals at night.

The *campero* carried your bedding and everything. Understand? But you took your two horses. Naturally. One day you'd use one and the next day the other.

You earned seventy-five cents a day . . . at the end of the trip. When we finished, we got paid. We'd leave here, from Guadalupe. Let's say we took two days; by the third day, we were already at the top of La Sierra. Or we could take two more days after we got there, branding, dehorning, or doing any other chore, until we were no longer needed.

Whenever we were dismissed, this Manuel, who was the boss, would take us to Cuba, like in the afternoon, so we could head on back the next day. There in Cuba, there we had a place to sleep and everything. He'd feed us, and come morning we'd head back from Cuba on our horses.

Well there was an opportunity to earn a little money so I'd go with him [Manuel Casaus]. Back in those days, you couldn't find a job for fifty cents a day. And if you could find a job to earn seventy-five cents a day, well, that's where you went, because there wasn't anywhere else.

Porfirio Romero, La Placita de Guadalupe, 1920. Courtesy
of Inesita Márez-Tafoya.

18 DE OCTUBRE DE 1979
Borracheras

¡Yo me llegué a poner algunas borracheras, eh, de mulas! ¿No te digo que una vez entré a caballo a la sala de don Porfirio en la Placita de Gualupe? Antonces había entrao yo de vaquero con un hombre que iba a llevar vacas paá pal Alto. Al fin me enojé y me arrendé. Y tenían un bautismo ai en el Cabezón, y yo y mi compañero que andaba conmigo, medio nos embolamos, ai en el Cabezón. Pues ya veníanos embolaos. Tocó que jue en papá y él se trujo mi caballo que usaba yo con la cama y todo. Y ya nos vinimos noche, yo y mi compañero, y haciéndose oscuro, ya

OCTOBER 18, 1979
Sprees

Why I, ah, really tied on some good drunks, with moonshine! Didn't I tell you that once I went on horseback to Don Porfirio's dance hall, on the plaza in Guadalupe. At that time I had just decided to become a cowhand, joining a man who was going to drive to a place called El Alto. After a while, I got mad and turned back. There in Cabezón a baptism was taking place, and I and my friend who was with me sort of got drunk. There in Cabezón. Why we were pretty loaded, in fact. It so happened that my dad went to Cabezón, and he brought back the horse that I was using for

estaba el baile a case del dijunto Porfirio. Pues entré hasta dentro de la sala en el caballo. ¡Todo borracho! Me agarró. Me *agarró* y me apeó del caballo, nomás que el caballo era muy pataleón.

Pero ese caballo, era malo el caballo, y pataleón, pero ese caballo yo lo hacía entrar a una casa. Ondequiera que le daba entraba ese caballo. Y era malo el caballo.

Oh, en ese tiempo tendría yo como diez y ocho años, quizás, y no, pus salieron todas las mujeres a juir (risas).

carrying my bedroll and everything. Night was coming on, it was already getting dark, and the dance was under way at the late Don Porfirio's house. Why, I went way into the dance hall on my horse. Dead drunk! Don Porfirio grabbed me. He *grabbed* me and brought me down off the horse, the only thing being that the horse was quite a kicker.

Why that horse was mean, and, as I say, quite a kicker, but that horse, I could make him go into a house. Anywhere I directed him, that horse would go in. And the horse was really mean.

I would say that back in those days, ah, I must have been about eighteen years old. Why, all those ladies took off running (laughter).

El caballo colorao

El caballo ese colorao. ¡Oh! Ése era un caballito un poco delgadito. Muy güen caballo, pero era muy reparador. ¡Muy cochino! Yo en la mañana le echaba la silla; le soltaba las riendas. Ése reparaba hasta que quería, pero asina lo dejaba yo y loo me subía en él, y ya no, pero ése reparaba cada vez de que le echaba yo la silla. ¡Oh! Un animal muy cochino. ¡Y *ligero*! Yo corría bestias mesteñas ai en la Mercé del Ojo del Espíritu Santo el día entero con ese caballo. ¡Bueno! Y güen pisador tamién. Ése no se volcaba. ¡A qué caballo oye! Ése lo crió en papá. Yo lo amansé, de las bestias que criaba en papá. Al fin se hizo viejo y lo vendí, porque se hizo viejo.

¡Oh sí! Ese caballo pa todo era güeno. ¡Pa todo! ¡Oh no! Era muy güeno. Y era muy güeno pa nadar en la agua ese caballo. Oh sí.

The Sorrel Horse

That sorrel horse. Oh! That horse was a small horse, a little bit on the thin side. A very good horse, but it was quite a bucking horse. Very mean! I would saddle it in the morning; I would let its reins loose. That horse would buck until it got tired, but that's what I'd let it do, and then I'd get on it, and then it'd stop, but that horse would buck every time I'd saddle it. Oh! A very mean horse. And *fast*! I would chase mustangs on that horse all day long there in the Ojo del Espíritu Grant. Good horse! And surefooted too! That horse never fell over. Listen, what a horse! Dad raised it. I broke it in, from among the horses Dad was raising. Finally it got old so I sold it, because it got very old.

Oh yes! That horse was good in everything. In everything! Oh yeah! It was very good. And that horse was a good swimmer. Oh yes.

Cattle Sanitary Board of New Mexico: 565

RE-RECORD

CERTIFICATE OF BRAND

I hereby certify that the following as shown on the cuts below and hereunto annexed, is a transcript of the brand and mark

LOCATION OF BRAND ON CATTLE

Left Ribs

LOCATION OF BRANDS ON HORSES, MULES AND ASSES

Left Hip

of   Mr. Nasario P. Garcia,   of   Cabezon,   Range.

in   Sandoval,   County and State of New Mexico. Recorded in State Brand Book

No. 2   , Page   30   , this   2nd   day of   October, 1931.

SECRETARY CATTLE SANITARY BOARD.
Albuquerque, New Mexico.

Certificate of brand issued to Nasario P. García, 1931. Courtesy of Nasario P. García.

18 DE OCTUBRE DE 1979
Entre todos juntaban las vacas

Pues, eh, cuando uno iba, güeno, comenzaré de este modo. Dígase que cuando uno iba a juntar las vacas pa marcar, llevaba uno campo y ponía uno campo en tal lugar. Y comenzaba uno a juntar vacas. Y loo de ai cambiaba uno su campo, y arreaba uno los animales que uno tenía a otro lugar a juntar más. Luego que ya juntaba uno los animales, pus antonces marcaba uno. Pero se estaba uno una semana o dos. Eso era todo lo que hacía uno.

OCTOBER 18, 1979
Together They All Rounded Up the Cattle

Well, ah, when one went, okay, let me start this way. Let's say that when you were going to round up the cattle for branding, you took camping gear and you set up in such and such a place. Then you started to round up the cattle. And then from there you moved your campsite, and you moved the animals you had to another place to round up some more. After you had rounded up the animals, well, then you branded. But you stayed one week or two. That's all you did.

En la tarde que llegaba uno . . . en la noche tenía uno que cocer frijoles, hacer comida. Güeno, frijoles, que es lo que . . . pero con carpas. Sí. Había munchas veces, eh, antonces casi en general no se usaban de llevar campos en carros y todo. En un caballo con la carga. Asina llevaba uno el campo, con un caballo o dos. Pero casi cada dos llevaban un caballo. O si iban compañeros, ai llevaban la cama; llevaban lonche y todo . . . Yo y mi hermano Ginio [Griego], yo me acuerdo, llevábanos un caballo, y ai llevábanos todo lo que necitábanos. ¡Todo! ¡Todo! En un caballo.

Cada quien como compañeros se juntaban y hacían toda la comida, porque ése era negocio de todos, aparte. Es diferente que cuando hay una compañía que pone los vaqueros y el cocinero y todo. Ai no. Cada quien tenía que hacer su negocio: su comida, atender sus caballos, y poner su carpa o lo que juera.

Munchas veces ni carpa llevaba uno. Aí nomás arriba de unas piedras, o arriba de una loma, aí tiraba uno todo y le pagaba el viento de todos rumbos.

Cuando estábanos ai en la mercé que se juntaba el Cabezón, San Luis y Gualupe, pus, ¡qué bárbaro! Había, pienso, como cincuenta vaqueros. Entre todos juntaban las vacas.

In the evening when you got to . . . at night you had to cook beans, fix supper. Okay, beans, which is what . . . but with tents. Yes. There were many times, ah, because back in those days, generally you weren't accustomed to taking camping gear in wagons and all that. You took your load on horseback. That's the way you took the camping gear, on a horse or two. But most of the time, for every two they packed one horse. Or if several partners went along, they took the bedding; they took lunch and everything . . . My "brother" Ginio [Griego] and I, I remember, would take one horse, and that's how we took everything we needed. Everything! Everything! On one horse.

Everyone like good buddies got together and cooked all the food because, apart from everything else, that was everyone's responsibility. It's a lot different from when there's a company that furnishes the cowboys and the cook and everything. Not there. Everyone had to do his part: cook his food, tend to his horses, and set up his tent or whatever.

Many times you didn't take a tent. There on top of rocks, or on top of a hill, that's where you threw everything down and the wind hit you from every direction.

When we were there on the grant, when Cabezón, San Luis, and Guadalupe got together, well, it was terrific! There were, I think, about fifty cowboys. Together they all rounded up the cattle.

30 DE MARZO DE 1982
Le sacó la silla la vaca

¡Oh! ¿Papá? ¡Déjate! A haste tú. Yo te voy a platicar.
Yo te voy a platicar. En, ai en el Empedrao, ¡oh, éranos
munchos; ai estábanos juntando las vacas cuando
primero entramos aá en el pasteo del BLM. Ai andaba
el Goodner; y estaban unos . . . estaba una cañada, y loo
estaba un arroyo aí. Y andaban lazando aí vacas, no sé
pa qué.

Andaba en papá en un caballito, mediano, un
caballito moro. Y, pues, eh, y loo se metió en papá y
lazó una vaca *grande*. La lazó. Cuando la lazó, partió la
vaca, y este caballo tenía idea de palancarse patrás.
Pues lo sacó contoy silla. ¡Por la cabeza! Le *sacó* la
silla la vaca (risas).

Allá andaba Macario Romero, y eran muy güenos
amigos.

—¡Ah qué don Teodoro!—le dijo.

—¡Qué!—le dijo [don Teodoro].—¡Qué se dejan de
estos gringos—dijía.

¡Oh!, y era güeno. ¡Oh! Venían como dos, pienso, y
le jerraron, y pasó [la vaca] onde él estaba, y era güeno,
y le puso el cabresto. ¡Le quitó la silla! ¡Sí! Le quitó la
silla al caballo . . . no, pus él sabía. Brincó de una vez,
¿ves? Uno tiene que estar muy liviano. El que sabe
andar a caballo tiene que cuidarse de todos modos. Sí.

The Cow Pulled Off His Saddle

Oh! Dad? Let me tell you! You'll see. I'm going to tell you a story. I'm going to tell you a story. Ah, there at el Empedrao, oh, there were lots of us; we were rounding up the cattle when we first came under the BLM pasturing system. There was Goodner, and there were these . . . there was a ravine and then there was also an arroyo. And there they were roping cows, I don't know what for.

Dad was riding a small, little horse, dapple-gray color. And, well, ah, and then he went and roped a *huge* cow. He roped it. When he roped it, the cow took off, and this horse had the bad habit of pulling up and digging in its hind legs. Well, the cow pulled him off, saddle and all. Over the horse's head! The cow pulled off his saddle (laughter).

Macario Romero was among the cowhands, and they were good friends.

"Oh Don Teodoro, you're something," he said to him.

"Hell," he [Don Teodoro] said to him. "Don't let these gringos up-stage you!," he'd say.

Oh, and he was good. Oh! There were two, I believe, and they missed the cow, and as it went by where he was . . . he was good, he roped it. The cow pulled off his saddle. Yes! It pulled off the horse's saddle . . . no, why, he knew how. He jumped off right away, see? You have to be very quick. The person who knows how to ride a horse has to be on the lookout for everything. Yes.

30 DE MARZO DE 1982
Se trozó la mano

[Don Juan José Griego y su papá] eran hasta parientes; eran primos. Pues yo sé, ah, poco, yo sé poco, ah, de cómo, cómo se trozó él [don Juan José] la mano. Él encerró un atajo de, eh, caballada en el corral allá en su rancho. Él andaba solo y se subió en otro caballo a lazar el caballo que iba a agarrar. Y era el día de San Pedro. Y cuando él lazó este caballo, ya juera que lo lazara del pescuezo o de las manos, o como quiera que sea, él traiba su cabresto amarrao a muerte en la silla. Se le enredó el cabresto en la mano. Y cuando lazó este caballo, este caballo le molió la mano.

Y luego de ai, reclamaban que él, lo que hizo que se jue [de la Sierra] como pudo, pa Salazar, a onde había gente que podía agarrar auxilio. Y allá había, estaban los Romeros, y ai llegó onde había auxilio. De ai no sé quién lo trairía [a Albuquerque] al doctor, o cómo, pero eso es lo que supe yo, que asina había pasao.

He Cut Off His Hand

They [Don Juan José Griego and his father] were even relatives; they were cousins. Well I know, ah, little, I know little, ah, as to how he [Don Juan José] cut off his hand. He penned up a herd of, ah, horses in the corral over on his ranch. He was by himself, and he mounted another horse to rope the horse that he was going to catch. It was Saint Peter's Day [June 29]. And when he roped this horse, whether he lassoed it around its neck or its front legs, or whatever, he had the end of his rope securely tied to his saddle. The rope got tangled up around his hand. And when he roped this horse, it chewed up his whole hand.

And from there, people claim that what he did was to go as best he could to Salazar [from La Sierra], to where there were people who could get help. And there was, there were the Romeros, and that's where he went to seek help. From there I don't know who must have brought him [to Albuquerque] to the doctor, or how, but that's what I found out. That's the way it happened.

19 DE MARZO DE 1992
Un golpeo

Güeno, voy a comenzar cuando iba mi hermano Ginio y mi hermana [Teodorita]. Iban de aquí de, de Alburquerque, paá pal rancho. Aá estaba yo y papá y mamá. Y, eh, mi hermano Ginio, que es mi cuñao, que era mi cuñao [ya es muerto], eh, tenía una troquita de esas Ford, que le pisan con el pie. Y iba otro conocido de él [en otra troca] que tenía gentes aá, en ese mesmo lugar de Gualupe. Y iban en la noche, y loo que ya pasaron la Ceja que iban, que pasaron el banco de la Ceja, pus había munchos, eh, . . . iba el camino curveando y había arroyos y tocó que ellos iban en la noche. Y había caido agua y se destruyó el camino. Hizo un golpeo, de maneras que ellos no vieron ese golpeo hasta que no llegaron. Ai se volcó la troca.

Y, eh, hermano Ginio no se hizo nada, pero mi hermana sí se lastimó poco. Y loo de ai el otro hombre que iba junto con ellos los llevó hasta Gualupe, a case de en papá. Y loo de ai jue, jue en papá al Cabezón y vido a este hombre Bernardino Hovey y vino y levantó a mi hermana y a mi cuñao y los trujo pacá pa la Plaza, al dotor.

Y lego yo y en papá tuvimos que venir en carro de caballos y jalar la troca pal rancho.

A Drop Off

Okay, I'm going to begin when my "brother" Ginio
[Griego] and my sister [Teodorita] were on their way,
they were on their way from here in Albuquerque,
heading for the ranch. That's where I and Dad and
Mom were. And, ah, my brother Ginio, who is my
brother-in-law, who was my brother-in-law, he had one
of those small Ford trucks, that you accelerate with a
foot starter. And there was another acquaintance of his,
a man [in another truck] who had relatives over there,
in that same place, Guadalupe. It was nighttime, and
then after they passed la Ceja, where there were many,
ah, . . . the road curved, and there were arroyos, and it
so happened that they were traveling at night. And it
had rained, and the road was destroyed. The rain
created a drop off, so that they didn't see that drop off
until they were right on top of it. That's where the
truck turned over.

And, ah, nothing happened to my brother Ginio, but
my sister did get hurt a little. And then from there, the
other man who was traveling with them took them to
Guadalupe, to Dad's house. And then from there, Dad
went to Cabezón and saw this man, Bernardino Hovey,
and he came and picked up my sister and my brother-
in-law and brought them to Albuquerque, to the doctor.

And then Dad and I had to come by horse wagon, to
pull the truck to the ranch.

Un granizal

Éste era en setiembre en 1936. Nos fuimos nosotros en la mañana; yo, mi esposa [Agapita García], en papá y mamá, pa otro rancho arrancar, eh, frijol. Y nos estuvimos hasta mediodía.

En esto empezó a nublarse y comenzó a cae agua, eh, pal rumbo de la Sierra. Venía caindo agua, y antonces, eh, nos dijo en papá; "Vale más irnos." Nosotros andábanos en carro de bestias y teníanos que caminar de allá del, de onde estábanos arrancando el frijol, a la casa. ¡Oh!, como cinco millas, quizás.

Pues de ai nos vinimos. Ya pa llegar quizás como una milla, antes de llegar a la casa, venía una nube, que no se vía. Oscura. Y comenzó la agua y luego en eso nos topó mi hermano, Antonio, y él traiba una lona.

Pues, eh, eh, cuando llegó la agua los metimos abajo del carro—lo tapamos con la lona, y en papá estaba teniendo los caballos, cuando en eso llegó un granizal, oye, que no poo dicir. Muy grande el granizo. A los caballos les estaba pegando y les levantaba, les levantó tamaños bordos. Cuando ya pasó el granizal, quedó blanco. Cuando llegamos a la casa, del lao que pegó el granizo, no dejó ventanas.

Pero nosotros nos metimos abajo del carro.

A Hailstorm

This was in September 1936. We took off in the morning; my wife [Agapita García], my dad and mom, to another ranch, to pick, ah, pinto beans. And we stayed until noon.

Meantime it started to get cloudy, and it began to rain, ah, toward La Sierra. The rain was coming, and then, ah, my dad told us: "We better go." We were on a horse wagon, and we had to travel from there, from where we were picking pinto beans, to the house. Oh!, about five miles, perhaps.

Well, from there we took off. Just about the time we were about to get home, about one mile, perhaps, a dark cloud was heading our way; you couldn't see. The rain started, and just about that time my brother, Antonio, met us, and he had a canvas.

Well, ah, ah, when the rain came, we got under the wagon—we covered ourselves with the canvas, while Dad was holding back the horses. About that moment a hailstorm hit. Let me tell you, I can't describe it. The hail was very big. The horses were being hit by the hail, and it was raising big welts on them. When the hailstorm was over, everything was white. When we got home, on the side where the hail hit, it left no windows.

But we got under the wagon.

Arroyo where Juan Valdez's body was discovered.

18 DE OCTUBRE DE 1979
La muerte de Juan Valdez

Te voy a contar de la muerte del dijunto Juan Valdez
del Cabezón. Éste, el dijunto Juan Valdez, era hombre
solo. Le quedaron dos de familia. Había Avelino, que le
decían, era el más grande. Y la muchachita, estaba
chiquita. Ella no supo nada, pero este Avelino sí. Es
que vido todo. Él estaba medio tonto. Pues habían
entrao dos una noche, con una vela, o con un farol,
pero más bien con una vela. Y onde estaba durmiendo
le dieron con una hacha. De ai lo sacaron, lo sacaron
arrastrando con un caballo, de la casa. Había un arroyo
que corría cerca de la casa, y lo sacaron y lo tiraron en

OCTOBER 18, 1979
The Death of Juan Valdez

I'm going to tell you about the death of the late Juan
Valdez from Cabezón. The late Juan Valdez was a
widower. He was left with two children [actually
three]. There was Avelino, as he was called. He was the
older. And the little girl; she was very small. She didn't
know what happened, but Avelino did. He presumably
saw everything, but he was a bit off his rocker. Well,
two men with a candle entered his house one night, or
perhaps it was a lantern, but more than likely it was a
candle. Right there where he was sleeping, they struck
him with an ax. From there they took him out, they

ese arroyo. ¿Y sabes tú dónde estaba esa casa? ¿Tú
sabes ónde abaja uno la Cuesta de Chihuahua, cuando
ya plano uno, pa aquel lao del Río Puerco, pa aquel lao
asina? Ai vivía el dijunto Juan Valdez. Al otro lao del
río, pal lao de la placita de Cabezón. Yo creo que
toavía ora se notarán ruinas de la casa.

Agarraron a los que lo mataron, porque Avelino los
entregó. Él supo quiénes jueron. ¿Quién sabe por qué
lo mataron?

Yo no estaba nacido toavía. Nomás oía pláticas de
hombres grandes cuando andábanos ai por todo ese
pais.

dragged him out of the house. There was an arroyo that ran close to the house, and they dumped him in it. And do you know where that house was? Do you know where the Cuesta de Chihuahua is, after you get to the bottom of the slope, toward the other side of the Río Puerco? That's where the late Juan Valdez lived. On the other side of the road, on the side where the village of Cabezón is located. I believe the ruins of the house are still visible today.

They caught the men who murdered him, because Avelino turned them in. He knew who they were. Who knows why they killed him?

I wasn't born yet. I only heard bits and pieces from older men, whenever we would go through all that part of the country.

18 DE OCTUBRE DE 1979
El dijunto Sotero

Una vez aquí en el Empedrao que le nombran, llegaron estos dos hombres, porque este hombre, el dijunto Sotero, tenía una laguna. Y ai llegaban los pasajeros, los que iban de aquí de la Plaza, de Alburquerque, pa que me entiendas, pal Río Puerco, y los que iban en carro de bestias y a caballo, ai paraban y les cobraba tanto el dijunto Sotero por dales agua. Asina vivía él. Y tenía cuarto pa los pasajeros allá en la casa onde vivía él.

En ese tiempo había un hombre ai, que estaba viviendo con él, que iba pasando. Güeno, llegaron éstos. Eran dos gringos, que sospechaban que el dijunto Sotero tenía dinero. Vinieron ya no sé a qué horas de la noche, y ai en la cama onde estaba le dieron un balazo. No sé en qué parte. Quizás pensaron que tenía dinero, pero no jallaron nada. De ai lo sacaron, y estaba un pino juera cerca de la casa, ai lo colgaron. Pero no lo horcaron; lo colgaron nomás. Quizás a ver si les dijiera si tenía dinero o no. El hombre este que estaba con el dijunto Sotero, quizás sintió todo. De ai, el hombre este, cuando vido lo que estaban haciendo, lo que habían hecho, salió corriendo a caballo y jue a dar parte. Y allá toda esa mesa pal otro lao de el Empedrao, ai vivía su hijo del dijunto Sotero. Cuando ya vino su hijo, junto con el hombre este que te digo, ya aquellos hombres que balearon al dijunto Sotero ya se habían ido. Su hijo lo jalló colgao patas pa arriba, pero toavía estaba vivo.

Ése era el dijunto Sotero de ai de el Empedrao.

The Late Sotero

One time here in El Empedrao, as it's called, these two men arrived, because this man, the late Sotero, owned a lake. And travelers used to stop there, those who were en route from Albuquerque, just so you understand what I'm saying, to the Río Puerco; and those on horse wagons or riding on horseback stopped there, and the late Sotero would charge them so much for water. That's how he earned a living. And he also offered lodging in the house where he lived.

At that time there was a man staying with him overnight, who was passing through. Well, then, these two men arrived. They were two *gringos*, who thought the late Sotero had money. They got there. I don't know what time of the night it was, but there where he was sleeping, they put a bullet in him. I don't know exactly where. Perhaps they thought he had money, but they found nothing. From there they dragged him out of the house. Close to the house there was a pine tree. That's where they hung him up, but they didn't kill him. They only hung him upside down. I guess they did it to see if he would tell them whether he had money or not. The man who was staying overnight with the late Sotero, I guess he heard everything. At that, this man, when he saw what they were doing, that is, what they had done, he took off on horseback to spread the word. On that mesa on the other side of El Empedrao, there lived the late Sotero's son. When his son arrived, along with this man I'm telling you about, the men who had wounded the late Sotero had already taken off. His son found him hanging upside down, but he was still alive.

That was the late Sotero from El Empedrao.

19 DE MARZO DE 1992
Floyd Lee

Güeno, yo no sé qué año sería, pero yo tenía, yo tenía
como diez y seis, diez y siete años. Yo estaba
trabajando de vaquero con este hombre que le dijían el
Magoy. Y ai onde andábanos juntando vacas, del patrón,
onde, onde yo estaba trabajando, estaba este Floyd Lee
de San Mateo, que tenía munchas vacas. Hombre rico.
Y un día nos encontramos con él, que él vino acá onde
andábanos juntando las vacas, a ver si no había vacas
de él. Y este hombre, reclamaban, este hombre, usaba
un paño aquí en la boca, amarrao. Y le pregunté a uno
de mis compañeros. Le dije:

—¿Por qué trae—le dije—un paño?

—Porque éste—dijo—no quiere a los mexicanos. Y no
quiere que le dé tufo de los mexicanos.

En San Mateo. ¡Oh, estaba rico! ¡Oh, tenía munchas
vacas!

Floyd Lee

Okay, I don't know what year it was, but I was, I was about sixteen, seventeen years old. I was working as a cowhand with this man whose name was Magoy. And there where we were rounding up cattle, belonging to the boss, where, where I was working, there was this Floyd Lee from San Mateo, who had a lot of cattle. Rich man. And one day we ran into him, because he came here to where we were rounding up cattle, to see if there weren't any of his cattle around. And this man, this man, people claimed he used a kerchief here, tied around his mouth. And I asked one of my buddies. I said: "Why is he wearing," I said to him, "a kerchief?" "Because," he said, "he doesn't like Mexicans. So he doesn't want the stink of Mexicans to get to him."

It took place in San Mateo. Oh, he was rich! Oh, he had a lot of cows!

30 DE MARZO DE 1982
Los Moras

Él [su papá] me platicaba a mí, eh, él trabajó con los Moras. Los Moras, don Vidal Mora, don Rafel Mora. No sé si don Juan Mora. Eran hombres ricos que tenían munchas vacas. Me platicó que él trabajaba de vaquero con ellos.

Y una vez salieron de allá de Gualupe con un atajo de borregas y cabras pal Condao de Lincoln. Y cuando llegaron aá al Condao de Lincoln, ai cambiaron borregas—no sé si llevaban hasta caballos, ai cambiaron borregas, lo que llevaban, por vacas. Y de allá trujieron muy güen atajo de vacas.

Me platicaba a mí que, que cuando, ya en la tarde, ya tenían todas las vacas y todo que iban arrendar patrás, es que de ai salieron ellos de, de tardeada que porque había gente muy mala ai, creo. Tenían que cruzar como una sierra; tenían que ir por un cañón. Y entraron en la tarde; ellos se vinieron de noche. Y is que toda la noche caminaron. Y is que salieron aclarando al otro día en el cañón, onde ya podían ir sin pena ninguna. Pero es que toda la noche caminaron. Traiban vacas. Caminando.

The Moras

He [his father] used to tell me, ah, that he worked for
the Moras. The Moras: Don Vidal Mora and Don Rafael
Mora. I don't know if for Don Juan Mora also. They
were very rich men, and they had a lot of cattle. He
told me that he worked as a cowboy for them.

One time they left from Guadalupe with a flock of
sheep and goats for Lincoln County. When they got to
Lincoln County, they traded sheep—I don't know if
they even took horses. There they traded sheep, which
is what they had, for cows. They returned with a very
good herd of cows.

My father would tell me that, that in the evening,
they already had the cows and everything they were
going to return with. They left from there well into the
evening, supposedly because there were, I believe,
mean people there. They had to cross like a mountain
ridge; they had to cross a canyon. And they entered the
canyon in the evening; they left at night. I understand
they traveled all night long; I understand they came
out of the canyon the next day as it was dawning,
where they were able to continue without any worry at
all. But I understand they traveled all night long. They
were bringing cows back. At a slow place.

Candelas de hielo

Güeno, pa, pa comenzar, éste era cuando estaba trabajando yo, por el, eh, el WPA en 1938. Teníanos campo, estábanos de campo, en la Placita de Cabezón. Y loo de ai veníanos del Cabezón a casa; de malas hay como siete o ocho millas. Y cuando nos tocaba comenzar como en la semana, yo venía de Gualupe al Cabezón a caballo.

Y salía a las cuatro de la mañana—era en febrero. Estaba tanto frío, oye, que cuando yo ya iba en medio camino, el resuello del caballo se le hacían candelas de hielo. Aí teníanos campo en el Cabezón, y ai los estábanos toda la semana hasta el sábado, y el sábado teníanos que irnos pa la casa.

En los sábados los íbanos de ai del Cabezón, que estábanos de campo, en la semana; los sábados los íbanos pa la casa, pa Gualupe. Y día lunes teníanos que madrugar par estar a las ocho en el Cabezón, pa que de ai nos levantaban las trocas pa ir a trabajar en el camino, eh, el camino que estábanos haciendo en del *highway* [44] hasta, hasta el Cabezón.

Había munchos [trabajando]. Dos de Gualupe. Estaban munchos. Todos iban . . . munchos si tenían carro, iban en carro. Si no tenías, tenías que ir a caballo . . . Oh no, ya cuando calentaba el tiempo pos, no era . . . lo duro era en el invierno. Enero, febrero y hasta marzo, porque en ese tiempo cayeron nevadas, hasta dos pies. Sí.

Agarraba toda la Cañada del Camino y por ai por la Laguna de don Ricardo, todo ese camino hasta el Cabezón.

Ice Candles

Okay, to, to begin with, this was when I was working for the, ah, the WPA in 1938. We had a camp, we were camping, in the placita of Cabezón. And then from there, we'd come from Cabezón home; maybe it's about seven or eight miles. And when it was time for us to get to work, like at the beginning of the week, I would go from Guadalupe to Cabezón on horseback. I would leave about four o'clock in the morning—it was in February. It was so cold, listen, that when I was halfway between Guadalupe and Cabezón, the horse's breath would turn into ice candles. That's where we had our camp, in Cabezón, and that's where we stayed all week until Saturday, and on Saturday we had to go home.

On Saturdays we'd go from there, from Cabezón, where we had our camp during the week; on Saturdays we'd go home, to Guadalupe. And come Monday, we had to get up early, to be in Cabezón at eight o'clock, because from there the trucks would pick us up to go work on the road, ah, the road that we were building from the highway [state road 44] up to, up to Cabezón.

There were many men working. Two from Guadalupe. There were many. They all went . . . many if they had cars, they went in a car. If you didn't have a car, you had to go on horseback . . . Oh, of course once it started to get warm, well, it wasn't . . . the difficult time was in winter. January, February, and even March, because back then we had some good snowstorms, up to two feet. Yes.

I would take the Cañada del Camino and go by way

En 1938, [ganaba] se me hace que treinta y ocho, treinta y ocho centavos la hora. En ese tiempo que yo estuve trabajando ai en el WPA, treinta y, treinta y ocho centavos la hora, ése era lo que los pagaban . . . estaba muy escaso el dinero. La gente estaba muy atrasada. Por eso es que pusieron esos trabajos del WPA, pa que la gente trabajara. Porque no podían depender de casi más de muy poquito de lo que tenían [en el rancho].

Cuando comenzaron, en el Cabezón. No. Cuando comenzaron lo pusieron [el WPA] ai en San Luis. Aí teníanos campo. Y loo de ai cuando ya avanzaron más adelante, cambiamos, eh, eh, campo pal Cabezón. Pus buscábanos una casa; había casas vacantes, vacías . . . Cuando sí pusimos carpas y too eso, que estábanos de campo ai en San Luis. Cuando comenzó.

Pues, eh, iban levantando el camino, componiendo ese camino. Lo levantaban, no con máquinas; con tiros de caballo. Con fresnos. Otros haciendo puentes. Jalando piedra y, y too lo que se ofrecía. Del *highway*, por San Luis, hasta el Cabezón, hasta cerca de la Sierra, la Sierra de San Mateo. Pa Gualupe no; no trabajaron ese camino. Y lo levantaron a juerza de fresnos y tiros de caballo.

[El gobierno] no daba nada [de comida]. Nosotros teníanos que poner la comida y todo. No daba nada . . . Pues, sí, nosotros teníanos que llevar comida por la semana . . . Yo y Antonio [su hermano] trabajamos ai en el WPA. Toda la gente esa de Gualupe, San Luis, Cabezón. Porque cuando hicieron ese proyeito de componer ese camino, acuparon la pura gente residentes de allí. Había unos que otros, pueda que troqueros o, o algunos como ingenieros de hacer puentes y todo eso, de otro lugar. Muy contaos de otros

of the Laguna de Don Ricardo, and take all that road until I got to Cabezón.

In 1938, I was earning I believe about thirty-eight, thirty-eight cents an hour. In those days, when I worked for the WPA, thirty-eight cents an hour, that's what they paid us . . . money was very scarce then. People were very poor. That's why they set up those WPA jobs, so that people could work. Because they couldn't depend on the very little subsistence that they had at the ranch.

When we started in Cabezón . . . when they started, they set up the WPA first in San Luis. That's where we had our camp. And from there, as they progressed farther with the road, we moved, ah, ah, the campsite to Cabezón . . . Well, we'd look for a house; there were empty houses . . . When we did set up tents and all of that, that's when we were camping in San Luis. When it started.

Well, ah, they were building the road, repairing that road. They were building it, not with machinery; with teams of horses, using scrapers. Others were building bridges, hauling rock and, and everything that was necessary. From the highway, through San Luis, to Cabezón, up to and close to La Sierra, La Sierra de San Mateo. Not to Guadalupe; they didn't build the road that way. And they built it by using scrapers and teams of horses.

The government didn't provide any [food]. We had to provide the food and everything else. It didn't give anything . . . Well, yes, we had to take food to last the entire week . . . Antonio [his brother] and I worked there for the WPA. All the people were from there in Guadalupe, San Luis, Cabezón. Because when they started that project, fixing that road, they hired only

lugares y partes. La mayoría era de todos lugares. Hasta Salazar. De San Luis hasta Salazar. Acuparon a toda la gente, pa dales trabajo. Casi, casi descogían a, a, en primer lugar al que tuviera muncha familia o estuvieran muy pobres y cosas asina.

No me recuerdo bien, pero yo creo que duró [el WPA] . . . duró fácil como un año, quizás. Cuando ya se acabó, ya no hubo WPA; por lo menos aá no hubo proyeitos.

the people, residents from there. There were some from here and there, perhaps the truckers, or some like bridge engineers and that sort of thing, who were hired from somewhere else. Very few from other places and parts [of the state]. The majority were from those places, including Salazar. From San Luis down to Salazar. They hired the people to give them jobs. They almost always, almost always selected, in the first place, those who had a large family or who were very poor and things like that.

I don't remember very well, but I believe it [the WPA] lasted . . . lasted more or less about a year, perhaps. When the work was over, the WPA ceased to exist, at least over there [in the Río Puerco Valley]; there were no more projects.

18 DE OCTUBRE DE 1979
Eran muy políticos

En papá, en papá y don Porfirio [Romero], en ese tiempo ellos eran muy políticos y estaban en el partido republicano. Había otros, pero los que casi estaban más ai en Gualupe, que tenían más juerza de política, eran el dijunto Porfirio y en papá.

[Los políticos] iban y echaban *speeches* aá. Como decía el dijunto . . . ¿cómo se llamaba, ¿cómo se llamaba este hombre?, era hermano de Filomeno, hombre, no me acuerdo cómo se llamaba. Ese hombre, ese hombre jue criao aá en Gualupe. Y cuando iba allá, decía, antes de comenzar a echar *speeches*, que "Cuando cada vez de que, cuando yo vengo aquí," decía, "cada vez de que miro los rastrojos," decía, que se acordaba de sus milpitas. Cuando vivía él aá, él llegó a sembrar y todo. Pero con eso salía él.

Pos, yo te diré, los [políticos] que, como ora . . . sí les llevaban dinero, ves, pero yo creo que . . . la mayor parte del dinero se quedaban con él. Algunos que otros les pasaban dinero pa *cambialos* [de un partido a otro], ¿ves? Pero había gente muy política que creiban en su partido, ya juera demócrata o republicano, o ni que les dijieran. Ellos iban [a votar]. El cuento es sostener el partido que llevaban. Y algotros que no les importaba, a ésos se les pasaban dinero, un peso o dos, y venían por ellos y los echaban a votar ai.

Ah, en ese tiempo casi había más republicanos. Ai se ganaba siempre los republicanos. ¡Siempre! Por eso era, yo creo, que nunca pusieron atención al demócrata, porque la mayoría era republicana. De manera que no les hacían muncho aprecio [a los demócratas].

OCTOBER 18, 1979
They Were Very Political

Dad, Dad and Don Porfirio [Romero], back then they were very political, and they belonged to the Republican party. There were others, but the ones who were almost always visible there in Guadalupe, who had more political pull, were the late Porfirio and Dad.

[The politicians] would go and make speeches over there. As the late . . . what was his name? What was this man's name?, he was Filomeno's brother. I don't remember what his name was. That man, that man was raised there in Guadalupe. And whenever he went there, he'd say, before starting his speeches, that "Every time I, whenever I come here," he'd say, "every time I see the stubbles," he'd say, that it reminded him of his little cornfields. When he lived over there, he got to plant and everything. But that's what he used to come out with.

Well, I'll tell you, these [politicians] who, like now . . . yes they took money to them, you see, but I believe that . . . the majority of the money, they [local politicians] kept it. They'd give money to some, here and there, to get them to change [parties], you see? But there were people who were very political, and they believed in their party, whether Democrat or Republican, so they didn't have to be told to vote. They went [on their own]. The thing was to support the party you belonged to. And others who didn't care, those were slipped money, a dollar or two, and they'd go after them, and they'd load them up to go vote.

Ah, back then almost everyone was a Republican. The Republicans always won. Always! That is why, I believe, they never paid attention to the Democrats, because the majority was Republican, so they didn't pay much attention [to the Democrats].

Don Bernardino Hovey

Güeno, yo te voy a decir. El dijunto Bernardino Hovey era un hombre muy político. Por años y años estuvo en la política. Me acuerdo yo, al último estuvo de alguacil mayor. Y él ayudaba a muncha gente, en diferentes modos, como podía. La gente de Gualupe, Cabezón y San Luis. Y la gente lo sostenía a él cuando corría en la política, porque hacía muncho por esos lugares él.

¡Déjame decirte! Más antes, antes de que controlara estos terrenos el BLM, acercaron la Mercé del Ojo del Espíritu Santo. Cuando ya acabaron de acercala, echaron todos, todos los animales pa juera. Porque ai era onde tenía la gente todos los animals sueltos, porque no estaba controlao. Estaba libre. Y los echaron pa juera. Cuando los echaron pa juera, que cerraron las puertas, pues, eh, tuvo que levantarse la gente, porque no tenía ónde mantener los animales. Y luego jueron, no sé si eso sería consejo de Bernardino o no, de que abrieran las puertas y soltaran los animales pa dentro.

Vinieron los del BLM y arrestaron a la gente por traspasar. Antonces Bernardino jue cabecilla y él jue el que habló por esa gente. Antonces, eh, arrestaron, pienso que arrestaron a este Bernardino. Y una mujer, no sé qué puesto tenía esa mujer, esa jue la que lo sacó.

Y por medio de esa revolución que hizo la gente, antonces tuvieron que dale permiso a la gente pa que entrara a la mercé. Pero no le dieron más de por tantos animales, no por todos, pa acomodar a toda la gente. Yo creo la idea de no dejar a todo el animalero que había salido, que tenía la gente, pa que no arruinara el lugar, el pasteo.

Don Bernardino Hovey

Okay, I'm going to tell you. The late Bernardino Hovey was a very political man. He was in politics for years and years. I remember that, toward the end of his career, he was sheriff. And he helped people in different ways, in any way he could. People from Guadalupe, Cabezón, and San Luis supported him whenever he ran for office, because he did a lot for those communities.

Let me tell you! Long ago, before the BLM controlled these lands, they fenced the Ojo del Espíritu Santo Grant. When they finished fencing it, they tossed all, all the animals out. That's where all the people had their animals loose, because the land wasn't under any control. It was unrestricted. And they tossed out, when they tossed them out, when they locked the gates, well, ah, the people had to rebel, because they didn't have a place to pasture their livestock. Then what they did, I don't know if it was on Bernardino's advice or not, was to open the gates and let the animals back in.

The officials from the BLM came, and they arrested people for trespassing. Then Bernardino took charge, and he's the one who spoke for the people. They, ah, they arrested, I believe they arrested this Bernardino. And a lady, I don't know what job that woman had, she's the one who bailed him out. And because of that revolt people made, then they had to give permission for the people to enter the grant. But they limited the number to so many animals. Not all of them, in order to accommodate all the people. I believe that the idea of not letting all the livestock back in that had been put outside the grant was so that it wouldn't ruin the pasture.

Birthplace of Nasario P. García, 1912. Photograph taken 1985.

27 DE SETIEMBRE DE 1990
Perdió muncho la gente

Pues sí, porque, ves, en ese tiempo que vino tan seco que perdieron munchos animales. Si una persona tenía tantas vacas y perdió y quedó con poquitas, con eso nomás le admitió el gobierno que entrara, como ora a la Mercé del Ojo del Espíritu Santo, onde estaba yo. Pero no lo dejaban arribar más. Ai lo tenían a uno y si se descuidaba y venía seco, lo reducían. En lugar de ir parriba, iba uno pa bajo.

Porque, por munchas cosas los que estaban manejando todo esto por el gobierno, querían orrar ai el zacate, que creciera. No querían animales demás, pa

SEPTEMBER 27, 1990
People Lost a Lot

Why yes, because, you see, back then when it got so dry, people lost many animals. If a person had so many cows and lost some and was left with a few, then that's how many the government allowed him, like for example, in the Ojo del Espíritu Santo Grant, where I belonged. But they wouldn't let you go up in numbers. They had you stuck there, and if you weren't careful and a drought came, they reduced you more. Instead of going up, you went down.

Because, for many reasons, those who were managing all of this for the government, they wanted to salvage

que arruinaran el zacate, pa proteger el terreno. Pues,
por un modo estaba güeno, pero pa la gente no estaba,
porque estaban limitaos. Nosotros llegamos a pelear
muncho porque diario, nomás venía seco, y le dicían [a
uno] que iban a reducir y lo dejaban a uno con una
cosita. Poca. "Y si se pone güeno," dicían, "les vamos
admitir estos animales patrás." Y al último puede que
la mitá admitieran. De manera que la gente, si venía
seco, la gente iba pa bajo. No podía levantar con sus
animales.

Pues munchos [rancheros] siguieron, pero tenían que
salir a trabajar, [porque] el gobierno no lo dejaba a uno
tener más que tantas [vacas]. Y luego cuando venía el
tiempo de los becerros, que nacían, tenía uno que
sacalos a los seis meses, ajuera, y vendelos. No podía
uno tenelos de seis meses, siete, ocho o que jueran
novillos, no.

Por eso jue que quitaron las borregas, porque ya
estaba quedando el, eh, el terreno que no era más de
tierra. En primer lugar quitaron todas las borregas. No
quedaron más de vacas. Oh, esos lugares no había más
de los terrones.

Por eso es que el gobierno se metió, pa proteger el
lugar, de que creciera la raiz del zacate y que hubiera
zacate. Güeno, viene de este modo. Como quiera que el
gobierno mandaba ese lugar; podía ser como le diera
gana. A eso le pareció al gobierno que sería güeno
proteger esos lugares pa que hubiera zacate; pus asina
lo hicieron. Pero pusieron unas reglas en un modo poco
malas, de que no le dieron chanza a la gente de que
arribara. Eso es lo más malo. No lo dejaban.

Bernardino [Hovey] hizo muncho por la gente. Hasta
lo encerraron en la cárcel, cuando cerraron la mercé,
que echaron todo el animalero; que se estaba muriendo,

the grass so it'd grow. They didn't want too many animals, because they would ruin the grass. They wanted to protect the land. Well, in one way it was good, but for the people it wasn't because their number of cattle was always reduced. We had to fight a lot, because quite certainly, as soon as it got dry, they'd tell you that they were going to cut down the number of cattle, and they left you with very little. Very little. "And if things get better," they'd say, "we're going to allow you to replace the reduced animals." Later on perhaps they admitted half [the reduced number]. So that people, if a drought came, people went backwards. People couldn't get ahead with the few animals they had.

Well, many [ranchers] continued [living there], but they had to go elsewhere to work, [because] the government didn't let you have more than a certain number of cattle. And then when calving season came, when they were born, you had to take them out of government pasture by six months of age, so you had to sell them. You couldn't have them from six, seven, or eight months of age to the time they were young bulls, no.

That's the reason they got rid of the sheep, because the land was turning into, ah, nothing but dirt. In the first place they cut out the sheep. The only thing left was cows. Oh, the only thing left in those places was the dirt clods.

That's the reason why the government intervened, to protect the soil, so the grass roots could grow, so there would be grass. Okay, this is the way it is. It doesn't matter, the government was in control of that place; it could do as it pleased. That's why the government thought it would be a good idea to protect those properties, so there would be grass; well, that's the way it was done. But they set up some rules that in one way were

¡no te digo! Que nos daban veinte y cinco pesos de dinero [al mes] pa que compráranos comida, y mandaban trocas del gobierno en el invierno pa que nos llevaran alfalfa cuando cerró la mercé, que la cercaron; la atrancó el gobierno. Pero pa que nos dieran permiso, por, por la residencia y por vivir tantos años la gente ai, y asina hacían la vida. Se entitularon que el gobierno era responsable, y que tenía que abrir esa, esa mercé pa que la gente entrara con sus animales.

Eso jue antes, si no estoy equívoco, pienso como el treinta y seis o el treinta y ocho, pienso. No sé. No me acuerdo. No me acuerdo de eso, pero no hacía muncho que me había casado yo. En ese tiempo toavía estabas tú chiquito.

El gobierno era responsable porque atrancó, cerró la mercé. ¡Oh! Vino la gente, hasta con rifles, a querer entrar. Y Bernardino [Hovey] jue el que se paró con la gente. Un bonche de veces. Lo arrestaron, a Bernardino. Lo encerraron en la cárcel. Los del gobierno. Y armaos y too. Pero Bernardino hizo muncho por la gente. ¡Oh! Toda esa gente perdió muncho con el gobierno. ¡Muncho! ¡Oh! Todo el tiempo. Todo el tiempo.

Y otra cosa que quería hacer en ese tiempo este Dennis Chávez—agarrar toda la mercé pa los indios. Ai jue otra pelea. No quería admitir a los mexicanos. Quería toda la mercé pa los indios, porque Dennis Chávez era el que representaba y hacía por los indios.

Y había otro senador tamién, muy cochino. Dennis Chávez y otro. No me acuerdo de su nombre de él. Pero el más cochino era este Dennis Chávez. Pero había un senador. No me acuerdo cómo se llamaba este senador. Hubo una junta ai en San Ysidro. Vino muncha gente. Antonces estaba el [Cas] Gooner [Goodner]. Enviamos cartas y todo. A mí me enviaron

bad, because they didn't allow people to better their lot.
That's the worst part. They deprived you of that.

Bernardino [Hovey] did a lot for the people. They even
jailed him, when the government locked up the grant,
when it pushed out all the animals; they were dying of
hunger. I'm telling you! They were giving us twenty-five
dollars [a month] so we could buy food, and the government would send trucks in the winter to bring us alfalfa
when it closed the grant, because it was fenced in; the
government locked it up. But in order for us to be given
grazing permits, because, because of our residency and
because people had lived many years over there, and
because that's the way we earned a living. We were
entitled to the government being responsible for the
people's well-being, which meant opening that, that
grant so that people could go in to pasture their
livestock.

This happened before, if I'm not mistaken, I believe
about thirty-six or thirty-eight, I believe. I don't know. I
don't remember. I don't remember that, but I hadn't
been married long. At that time you were very small.

The government was responsible, because it locked
up, it closed the grant. Oh! People came, some even
carrying rifles, to gain entrance. And Bernardino [Hovey]
was the one who stood up for the people. A bunch of
times. They arrested him. They put him in jail. Those
from the government. And they were armed and all. But
Bernardino did a lot for his people. Oh! All of those
people lost a lot with the government. A lot! Oh! All
the time. All the time.

And another thing that this Dennis Chávez wanted to
do at the time—take the entire grant for the Indians.
That was another fight. He didn't favor Hispanos. He
wanted all of the grant for the Indians, because Dennis

cartas. Y este senador me envió una carta muy, ¡uh!.
¡Injuriándome! Ya estaba cerca de la eleción. "Yo," dije,
"éste por obra de Dios," dije yo, "le pase una cosa."
¡Muérese antes de la eleción! Sí. Se murió antes de la
eleción, y andaba corriendo otra vez de senador. Y se
murió. Como en el cuarenta, por ai.

Pero Dennis Chávez no hacía por los mexicanos. Por
los indios. Quería toa la mercé, pa los indios. Y al fin
vino de que . . . ¡Uh! ¡Cuba! ¡Todos! Íbanos a San
Ysidro, a juntas, y en dondequiera, a pelear, y al fin nos
dejaron una orilla. Del *highway* pacá es de los indios
. . . Y a nosotros nos dejó pallá.

Nada más que nosotros entramos con los permisos,
que entramos y por la posesión que ya éranos criaos en
ese lugar y asina hacíanos la vida. La única cosa que
cambió el gobierno, que teníanos el derecho de vender
el permiso. No en terreno, pero nos dio chanza de que
podíanos vender el permiso, lo cual es una cosa de lo
mejor que podía haber hecho . . . y otra cosa, que no
podíanos vendérselo a otras personas ajuera, como de
Texas, Colorao o companías; pero perdió muncho la
gente.

Chávez was the one who represented and did a lot for the Indians.

And there was another senator, very nasty. Dennis Chávez and this other senator. I don't recall his name. But the worst one was this Dennis Chávez. But there was a senator. I don't remember what his name was. Anyway, there was a meeting there in San Ysidro. A lot of people showed up. At that time [Cas] Goodner was around. We had sent letters and all. They also sent me letters. And this senator sent me a letter, uh! Insulting me! Elections were just around the corner. "I," I said to myself, "through the grace of God, I hope something happens to him." He died before the elections! Yes. He died before the election, and he was running for reelection. And he died. This was about forty, thereabouts.

But Dennis Chávez didn't do anything for his people. For the Indians, yes. He wanted the entire grant for them. It finally got to the point that . . . Uh! Cuba! Everyone! We'd all go to meetings in San Ysidro, wherever, to fight, and the government finally gave us a section of the grant. From the highway this way [toward Cabezón Peak] belongs to the Indians, and from there on to us.

The only thing is that we went into the grant with the permits we had, because of the fact that we had been raised there in that country, and because that's the way we earned our living. The only thing the government changed was the right for us to sell the permit. Not the property. The same thing as I did. That was a good thing the government did for us. I sold the permit. Not the land, but we were given a chance of selling the permit, which is the best thing the government could have done for us . . . and another thing, we couldn't sell it to strangers, like from Texas, Colorado, or companies; but people still lost a lot.

Glossary

REGIONAL	STANDARD

A

aá	allá
acabábanos	acabábamos
a case (de)	en casa (de)
acercala	acercarla
acupaba	ocupaba ("would hire")
acuparon	ocuparon ("hired")
aflotalo	frotarlo
agradecele	agradecerle
agüelo	abuelo
a hasta tú	ya verás tú
ai	allí
aí	allí
aigre	aire
ajuera	afuera
a juerza de	a fuerza de
Alburquerque	Albuquerque
alcojólicos (as)	alcohólicos (as)
alfarfa	alfalfa
algotros	algunos otros
almorzar	desayunar
amarrao	amarrado
a más de	además de
anancas	en anancas
andábanos	andábamos
animalero	animales ("a bunch of")
antonces	entonces
aprevenía	prevenía
aprevenidos	prevenidos ("prepared")
araos	arados
armaos	armados
arrancalo	arrancarlo
arrendar	volver
arrendé	volví

REGIONAL	STANDARD
asegún	según
asina	así
atendelos	atenderlos
atrás	detrás
ayudale	ayudarle
ayudanza	ayudante(a)
ayudao	ayudado

B

REGIONAL	STANDARD
bajo	abajo
bestias	caballos
bordos	verdigones ("welts")
buscábanos	buscábamos

C

REGIONAL	STANDARD
caiba	caía
caido	caído
caindo	cayendo
camalta	cama
cambialos	cambiarlos
cantidá	cantidad
carpas	tiendas
celes	hacerles
cequia	acequia
coletaba	colectaba
coletas	colectas
colgao	colgado
colorao	colorado
companía (s)	compañía (s)
componiendo	arreglando
comprábanos	comprábamos
compráranos	compráramos
contaos	contados
contoy	con todo y
controlao	controlado

REGIONAL	STANDARD
corretiaban	correteaban
corretiar	corretear
cortábanos	cortábamos
costumbraba	acostumbraba
creiban	creían
creyen	creen
crianza	respeto
criaos	criados
criatura	niño(a)
Crismes	Navidad
cuartito	dispensa
cuasi	casi
cuenta	cosa
cuidao	cuidado
cuñao	cuñado

Ch

chanza	oportunidad
charolas	bandejas
chiche	pecho

D

dale(s)	darle(s)
de malas	más o menos
demasana	damasana
deputao	deputado
desbaratao	desbaratado ("broken")
descalofrío	escalofrío
descogelas	escogerlas
descogían	escogían
despachar	mandar ("to send")
desparecieron	desaparecieron
destendidos	extendidos
dicían	decían
dicir	decir

REGIONAL	STANDARD
dijía	decía
dijían	decían
dijiera	dijera
dijieran	dijeran
dijieron	dijeron
dijirte	decirte
dijunto	difunto
dionde	donde
diónde	dónde
diondequiera	dondequiera
dotor	doctor
dotores	doctores

E

REGIONAL	STANDARD
echale	echarle
edá	edad
ejecutalos	disciplinarlos ("to discipline")
ejecutar	disciplinar
eleción	elección
embolaban	emborrachaban
embolaos	embolados; borrachos
empedrao	empedrado
enbrujao	embrujado
encerrábanos	encerrábamos
encerraos	encerrados
enchorraos	enchorrados ("lined up")
engolvía	envolvía
enpachaos	empachados
en papá	mi papá
enparejaba	enfrentaba
en primo(a)	mi primo(a)
ensolvaba	ensolvía
ensolve	sobrante ("water residue," i.e., sticks, etc.)
enterrao	enterrado
entrao	entrado
entregale	entregarle

REGIONAL	STANDARD
enyerbao	enyerbado
equívoco	equivocado
éranos	éramos
escusao	escusado
esperencia	experiencia
esplicar	explicar
estábanos	estábamos
este	esto
estógamo	estómago
exaito	exacto

F

fácil	tal vez
figurábanos	figurábamos
fletiaba	fleteaba
floja	suelta

G

garrale	agarrarle
gaselín	gasolina
Ginio	Higinio
golpiaban	golpeaban
granizal	granizo ("hailstorm")
Griavelita	Gabrielita
Gualupe	Guadalupe
güelta	vuelta
güen	buen
güena(s)	buena(s)
güeno(s)	bueno(s)
güevo	huevo

H

hablale	hablarle
hacíanos	hacíamos

REGIONAL	STANDARD
hijadero	ahijadero
horcaron	ahorcaron

I

íbanos	íbamos
inflencia	influenza
is que	es que

J

jallaron	hallaron
jalló	halló
jerraron	erraron
jirvían	hervían
jirviendo	hirviendo
jonda	honda
jue	fue
juera	fuera; afuera
jueran	fueran
juéranos	fuéramos
jueron	fueron
juerte	fuerte
juerza	fuerza
juir	huir
juisque	aguardiente
jumazos	humazos
jumo	humo
juntas	reuniones
juquiaron	escarbaron
juventú	juventud

K

L

lao	lado

REGIONAL	STANDARD
lazao	lazado
lego	luego
levantábanos	levantábamos
levantala	levantarla
levantao	levantado
limitaos	limitados
liniaba	alineaba
liviano	ligero
lonche	almuerzo
loo	luego
los	nos
lotra	la otra
lotro	el otro

LL

llegábanos	llegábamos
llevala	llevarla
llevales	llevarles

M

machucaban	machacaban
machucaran	machacaran
manejaban	dirigían
manias	manías
maiz	maíz
marcaos	marcados
medianito	chiquito
mediano	chico
mentao	mentado ("popular")
mercé	merced
mesmo	mismo
mestra	maestra
midían	medían
mitá	mitad
mono	muñeco

REGIONAL	STANDARD
moquetes	puñetazos
muncha(s)	mucha(s)
muncho(s)	mucho(s)
muría	moria
muriría	moriría
murre	muy

N

naiden	nadie
navajiaban	navajeaban
necitaban	necesitaban
necitábanos	necesitábamos
noche	tarde
nomás	sólo; solamente
novedá	novedad
nuevas	noticias

Ñ

O

ocupaba	empleaba
ocupaos	ocupados
onde	donde
ónde	dónde
ondequiera	dondequiera
onque	aunque
oportunidá	oportunidad
ora	ahora
orilla	sección
orraba	ahorraba
orrar	ahorrar
otubre	octubre

REGIONAL	STANDARD

P

REGIONAL	STANDARD
pa	para
paá	para allá
pacá	para acá
paceles	para hacerles
pal	para el
palancarse	apalancarse
pallá	para allá
pal rumbo	para el rumbo
papases	papás
pa que	para que
paquel	para aquel
par	para
parao	parado
parriba	para arriba
partió	se fue; salió
pasao	pasado
pasaos	pasados
patrás	para atrás
pedile	pedirle
peliaban	peleaban
piones	peones
plebe	muchachos ("kids")
podíanos	podíamos
polquiar	polquear
pompiaban	pompeaban
poo	puedo
pos	pues
proyeito(s)	proyecto(s)
pus	pues

Q

REGIONAL	STANDARD
quemao	quemado
quitábanos	quitábamos
quitale	quitarle

REGIONAL	STANDARD

R

raiz	raíz
recomunir	reconvenir
remudaban	cambiaban
reparaba	respingaba
reparador	bronco
resfriaos	resfriados
retiraos	rctirados

S

sacalas	sacarlas
sacale	sacarle
sacalos	sacarlos
salao	salado
salíanos	salíamos
Santana	Santa Ana
sentidos	oídos
setiembre	septiembre
siguía	seguía
solevaos	solevados
sostener	mantener
sostenía	mantenía
subíanos	subíamos
sujetar	detener ("to restrain")

T

tamaños	grandes
tamién	también
tantas	cuantas
tantos	cuantos
tapale	taparle ("to cover")
tapar	cubrir
tardábanos	tardábamos
tardáranos	tardáramos

REGIONAL	STANDARD
tardeada	tarde
tenelos	tenerlos
teníanos	teníamos
teniendo	deteniendo
teta	chupete ("pacifier")
toa	toda
toavía	todavía
tomulto	tumulto
too	todo
topar(nos)	encontrar(nos)
tostao	tostado
traiban	traían
trainos	traernos
tresquila	trasquila
tresquilando	trasquilando
trocas	camionetas
troqueros	camioneros
troquita	camioneta ("small truck")
troteaba	trotaba
trujieron	trajeron
trujo	trajo
tuallas	toallas
túnicos	vestidos
tuviéranos	tuviéramos

U

umentos	aumentos; barandillas ("sideboards")
usábanos	usábamos
Utimia	Eutimia

V

vendelos	venderlos
veníanos	veníamos
verdá	verdad

REGIONAL	STANDARD
vía	yeía
vide	vi
vido	vio
vinir	venir
vites	viste
vivíanos	vivíamos

W

X

Y

yeleras (hieleras)	neveras, refregiradores

Z

zalellería	zalearía

Modismos/Idioms

A

Spanish	English
A echar carreras	To race (horse races)
Agarraron más alas	They became wiser
Ai daban la güelta	That's where they turned around
Al rato	A short while later
A mí se me hace que	I believe that
A muerte	Firmly
A poquito de que se metiera el sol	A little after sunset

B

C

Spanish	English
Casa por casa	From house to house
Comenzó a cae agua	It started to rain
Conforme les juera tocando	According to their own fate
Corretiar las vacas cuando nos tocaba	To go after the cows when it was our turn
Cuando tocaba que hacían baile	When it happened that they had a dance
Cuando yo ya tuve edá	When I was old enough

CH

D

Spanish	English
Daban güelta con su procesión	They went around (the placita) with their procession
De güenas a primeras	All of a sudden

SPANISH	ENGLISH
¡Déjate!	Wow! No kidding!
De malas	About, more or less
De tardeada	Late in the evening
De todos modos	In any case
De una vez	Right away
De vez en cuando	From time to time
Día por día	Day after day

E

Echaban pan	They baked bread
El cuento es que	The fact is
En eso	About that time
En esto	About this time
Entraban hechos espuelas y chaparreras	They went in wearing spurs and chaps
Entre el día	During the day
En vez en cuando	Once in a while
Era muy mentao	He was well-known
Eso jue años, años	That was years ago

F

Fácil que sea lo mesmo	Perhaps it's the same
Fácil tendría más de diez y seis años	Perhaps I was more than sixteen years old
¡Fíjate tú!	Just imagine!
¡Fíjate tú cuantos años hace!	Just imagine how long ago that was!

G

H

Había caido agua	It had just rained

SPANISH	ENGLISH

I

Iba a un tiempo	One time

J

Jue a dar parte	Went to spread the word

K

L

La gente estaba muy atrasada	People were very poor
La mayor parte	The majority
Le echaba la silla	He would saddle (the horse)
Le echaban lumbre al horno	They'd start up a fire in the bee-hive oven
Les daba aigre	They suffered from drafts
Loo van a la novedá	Right away they'd go find out what happened

LL

M

Muy contada la vez	Very rarely

N

No les hacían muncho aprecio	They didn't pay much attention to them
Nomás las puras mujeres	Only the women

SPANISH	ENGLISH

Ñ

O

P

¡Pa que mires tú!	Just imagine!
Pero pasó, pasó	But it came and went
Por medio de	By dint of
Pueda que	Perhaps
Pus quería acabar con todo	Why, he wanted to tear everything up

Q

¡Qué bárbaro	Good gracious!
¡Qué pueden haber sido!	Who knows what they were!
Quería acabar con la casa	He wanted to tear up the house

R

S

Sacaban las Estaciones	They celebrated the Stations of the Cross
Se iban derecho a	They headed straight for
Se lo troteaba el perro al toro	He'd set the dog on the bull

T

Tener cuidado con	To take care of
Tenía manias	It had tricks
Tiros de caballos	Teams of horses

SPANISH	ENGLISH
Tocó que ellos iban en la noche	It so happened they were going at night
Tocó que jue en papá	It so happened that my dad went

U

Uno atrás de otro	One right after the other

V

Vale más irnos	We better go
Venía caindo agua	It started to rain

W

X

Y

Ya se acabaron	They're all gone
Yo me llegué a poner algunas borracheras	There were times when I got so drunk
¡Y ya era hombre grande!	And he was already an old man!

Z